In the Company
of Children

In the Company of Children

Horace Puglisi

authorHOUSE®

AuthorHouse™
1663 Liberty Drive
Bloomington, IN 47403
www.authorhouse.com
Phone: 1-800-839-8640

Published by AuthorHouse   05/02/2013

ISBN: 978-1-4817-4546-8 (sc)
ISBN: 978-1-4817-4545-1 (hc)
ISBN: 978-1-4817-4544-4 (e)

Library of Congress Control Number: 2013907756

Table of Contents

Part VI: Closing Comments

Part VII: Appendices

Dedication

On Friday, December 14, 2012, twenty young children and six staff members were brutally murdered at Sandy Hook Elementary School in Newtown, Connecticut. The lives of these children, ages six and seven, were cut short. They will never experience the joys and love so abundant in our schools, nor will they experience all of the challenges and rewards found in our schools. This book, *In the Company of Children,* is dedicated to their memory. I offer you a glimpse of my teaching experiences in an elementary school classroom as a way to celebrate the *good* our schools offer our children.

—Horace Puglisi, Ph.D.

Introduction

In the Company of Children is an invitation to read about my beliefs about teaching and learning. By including dozens of classroom photos, I share the varied ways I used to encourage children to become investigators; help them discover their innate abilities; guide them to set meaningful goals; show them the value of accuracy, attention to detail, and diligence; provide ways for them to develop deep-seated friendships; and establish genuine family relationships in the classroom.

For me, the most effective kind of teaching takes its cue from the understanding that children are natural active learners. They are able to construct new knowledge from real experiences and store these new experiences into their already existing mental frameworks. Each student has his or her own idiosyncratic mannerisms, needs, and learning style. In the classroom, students are constantly making decisions, becoming participants in their own education. Each is part of a community of learners, coming to understand ideas from the inside out with one another's help. They all still acquire important facts and skills, but in the context of a "big picture" and for a purpose they understand. Often, their questions drive the curriculum for the day or the whole week. They discover that learning to think like scientists, writers, and historians matters most.

Throughout this narrative you will read personal statements written by my students. I incorporate these testimonials because they represent the passion these children have for learning and the satisfaction it brings them, and they show my students' reactions to my beliefs put into practice.

This book is divided into six sections. The first, Early Beginnings, takes you back to my earliest teaching experiences and illustrates the very first significant eureka moment I had regarding teaching. Part II includes some of my basic beliefs about teaching—I write about friendship, teamwork, and total focus. Part III is about the big-picture themes and corresponding units. I describe the Sons and Daughters of the Galileo Society and the World's Great Explorers units. Part IV focuses on some of our special events, such as Halloween Madness and Marshmallow Accelerators. Part V illustrates how I incorporated the school curriculum—literacy, mathematics, and science. Part VI includes my final comments about teaching and learning.

—Horace Puglisi, PhD

He is Mr. Possible,
the one who helped us get even more creative.
A bear that teaches his cubs to become wise with
wisdom.
He is the GPS of our lives, that which tells us to take
the right steps to live in peace.
He is the fire that won't go out when teaching.

—Alex Souvannaseng

Acknowledgements

Teaching is not and should not be a solitary profession. Educators need to reach out to colleagues so they can join forces and work in partnerships. Six individuals—Debbie Richardson, Paul Garrett, Kathy Grace, Judy Kaplan, Ellie Morency, and Colleen Armstrong—were my teammates during my final years teaching in Vermont. Together we were able to fashion and invent unique learning opportunities for the children.

Above is a photo of Judy Kaplan (media center director) dressed as Queen Isabella during a Columbus voyage reenactment. Judy and I planned the school's first Invention Convention program; we, along with other media personnel, traveled to Boston and were invited for a behind-the-scenes tour of the Children's Museum. Later, we designed and added various physical learning structures in the media centers. These structures were modeled after those observed in Boston.

When the Montreal Botanical Society learned about my plans for including the University of Vermont's (UVM) botanical observatories in a new integrated botany unit—Lessons of the

Rain Forest—they shipped a huge collection of semitropical plants. Judy found space in her media center, where we displayed dozens of these plants using the many National Gardening Association GrowLabs I had purchased with funds from my National Science Foundation (NSF) Science Teaching Award. Later, she provided a large space where I created an indoor vivarium full of tropical plants, sheltered by polyurethane walls and featuring paintings done by Liz Sidi. Years later when I was asked to add reading to my instruction, Judy introduced me to the huge Dorothy Canfield Fisher (DCF) collection, and we both assembled a reading list incorporation the themes I had planned to include in my reading program (please see Appendix D).

In the photo below, Colleen Armstrong, UVM greenhouse director, helps one of my students locate and observe seed development during one of our UVM field study labs. Colleen planned the students' experiments and arranged for us to use two houses of the huge greenhouse for our Lessons of the Rain Forest unit. Ellie Morency, art teacher, accompanied our two classes and instructed students on drawing the various semitropical plants at the UVM greenhouse one day a week for six weeks.

Above is a photo of Paul Garrett, technology teacher. Paul and I collaborated on my first big-theme unit—Sons and Daughters of the Galileo Society. Paul introduced me to and coached me in LinkWay. We also worked closely together instructing my students in Microsoft Logo during my geometry units. Paul assisted me with various student PowerPoint presentations during my career at Founders Memorial School.

Debbie Richardson was my teammate for six years. She combined her expertise in writing with my skills in science and math. Together, we created Lessons of the Rain Forest, Sons and Daughters of the Galileo Society, and World's Great Explorers. Our bond was sealed with a "silent oath" that we would take on these projects no matter the challenge.

During my last year teaching while I was on a long sick leave, Debbie met with my students to assist them in writing eulogies expressing their memories of me. Several are included in this story.

What we come to believe and accept is a product of how each of us uses our senses and beliefs to interpret both the physical and metaphysical world.

Each of us perceives, reacts, and learns in our own unique way.

As educators, it is our ethical and moral responsibility to acknowledge the uniqueness of each individual child and to celebrate each student's potential to contribute to the future of our society.

—Horace Puglisi

PART I

The Early Beginnings

CHAPTER 1

❖

Tuning in to the Right Channel—What I Learned from Other Educators

With today's TV remote control, most if not all TV viewers surf stations to "see what's on." Brief reflection will illustrate that there are dozens of varied programs—but only a few of these capture our attention. A classroom full of twenty or so fifth graders can be tuned to twenty different channels. A teacher, when giving a lesson where *all* of the students *must* tune in to the same channel, may find the task unmanageable, if not unreasonable. I recall that during my first two years as a Peace Corps teacher, 1964-66, all of my teaching was "instructional." All of my students were required to focus on *one* concept or idea and somehow organize in their minds those facts, whether or not they were engaged or able to connect the new thoughts to their own experiences. This approach worked quite well, as the students were interested only in details and facts that would help them successfully pass their British exams.

My attention was *not* on how my students learned or on how to transform a classroom into a *family* of learners intent on helping, collaborating with, and supporting one another. My beginning teaching years were quite different from my later years.

How do we change our attitudes and behaviors? In education, the common method is for a supervisor to observe a teacher, make notes, and offer recommendations about changes. For me, personally, these methods brought little satisfaction. My personal changes in teaching came from unintended events. While completing a full year of advanced graduate studies at the University of Maine, Orono, 1972-73, I enrolled in a course taught by Assistant Dean Jim Muro. The course was based on William Glasser's philosophy of reality therapy.

It was there that I learned that all of us have five basic needs: *power*—feeling a sense of achievement and feeling worthwhile; *love and belonging,* which include having friends in the classroom; *freedom*—having autonomy and one's own space; *fun*—feeling pleasure and enjoyment while learning; and *survival*—seeking both physical and emotional nourishment as well as comfort. I brought my understanding of these needs to my position as an assistant principal in Southborough, Massachusetts. One of my responsibilities was student discipline. Applying Glasser's principles was challenging in some circumstances, as most teachers viewed my role as that of chief disciplinarian. However, when I asked the children who were sent to me, "What do you want from school? What are you doing in class to get what you want? Is it working?", those children perceived me as someone trying to help them rather than punish them. For the remainder of my teaching career, I carried William Glasser's notion with me.

I had another eureka moment in 1980 while I was completing my doctoral residency at the University of Connecticut. I had been taking courses with Professor Anthony Gregoric, who had written extensively about learning styles. It was then that I began to understand those mediating forces that influence how children learn. I had little knowledge of learning styles. Through the insights of Dr. Gregoric, I became acquainted with my own mediating style and learned how I differed from other educators. It was clear to me that I had no awareness of, not even a clue about, how students' learning styles could affect not only how they learned, but also what they learned. I was making progress and learning more and more about teaching.

I also learned from Professor Gregoric a triad model of teaching. This model illustrates that an effective teacher focuses on education, teaching, and instruction. Below is an illustration of Dr. Gregoric's model.

Teach

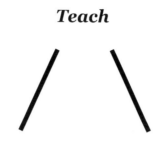

Educate   *Instruct*

In its simplest form, *teaching* is exposing those values and beliefs held by a teacher to his or her students. *Educating* means revealing to students the "big picture" of what they are studying, and informing students that what they are learning has many facets. *Instructing*—which has been the traditional form of teaching—simply means telling students about basic facts or strategies. In further chapters, I will share examples of *teaching, educating,* and *instructing.* The integrated units—Sons and Daughters of the Galileo Society (SDGS)—represent my effort to *educate* students to see the big picture of how science has changed over time. A second study, the World's Great Explorers, gave the children the opportunity to understand those qualities shared by many of our explorers.

PART II

My Beliefs about Teaching

CHAPTER 2

❖

Friendship—Love Is Most Important

What are children looking for when they arrive at school? The answer is clear: friendship. All of us have the capacity to feel love, and we have the ability to build long-term relationships with friends. Because children have this innate capacity to form cooperative relationships, the classroom becomes the prime location for friendships to grow and flourish.

Opportunities for students to bond together, help one another, and develop ways to form new relationships are critical for children's development. As friendships develop, the classroom evolves and becomes a family. And, eighteen to twenty separate individuals develop a singularity of purpose and learn that love is most important. This aphorism is often expressed in *Tuesdays with Morrie* by Mitch Albom. Children begin to perceive that their classmates are family. Cooperation and love becomes the standard. Conflict and competition diminish and, in many cases, become nonexistent.

How does a teacher facilitate enduring friendships? By designing learning situations wherein students are free to observe each other's actions and by giving them spontaneous opportunities to suspend their own activity in favor of assisting a friend. The classroom becomes an enterprise where students are making decisions about whom they will cooperate with and how much time they need to complete a certain task. There is freedom of movement. The teacher does *not* control the students' rate of learning nor the depths of their understanding.

The teacher encourages children to ask more probing questions; develop the desire to produce high-quality output; and, most important, develop a personal value system by which they abide. Much of their learning is based on their own motivations, interests, and abilities.

Two young scientists and two young explorers share their delight and friendship during the Sons and Daughters of the Galileo Society's History of Science Fair and the World's Great Explorers Fair.

The seeds of a lasting relationship can be planted in the classroom. However, it takes months for these friendship bonds to develop. When students are given work that demands their mutual attention, and when one student gives attention and love to another, then the other is obliged to offer the same. Below, two girls share their delight and companionship during our World's Great Explorers Fair.

Good teachers do much more than instruct children. They develop a relationship built on trust, honesty, humor, and, above all, love. This photo was taken during our annual SDGS History of Science Fair. The young boy selected Archimedes as his scientist.

Too often we fail to recognize the value of friendships that are buoyed up by the brotherhood or sisterhood among children. There is a force that flows between them, an invisible understanding cementing their friendship.

Just thinking about a friend makes you want to do a happy dance, because a friend is someone who loves you in spite of your faults. —Charles Schulz

"Everybody needs one essential friend."
—William Glasser

We all want a few kind words, a feeling of reassurance. Friendship makes that offering. It also has restorative powers for children who were looking for that essential friend.

How do we encourage friendship in the classroom?

Sharing knowledge offers each teacher a glimpse into a child's world. I'm not speaking about classroom knowledge, but about the child's own personal experiences and learning beyond the classroom. Informal settings, whether classroom meetings, luncheons, or recess walks with students, provide opportunities for teachers to gain insights into each student's personal attitudes and beliefs. Do we take the time to explore some of our students' deepest attitudes? Taking time to visit the children during recess or while they're having lunch in the cafeteria may provide teachers an opportunity to learn about students' behaviors and attitudes outside the classroom.

Helping others brings our children much closer together. When you *help* someone, you establish a bond that speaks to the needs both of you have. We can learn from each other, especially if the language we hear makes sense to us. I believe children speak to each other in a way that is easy to understand. And the one who conveys knowledge achieves a personal sense of satisfaction for having helped a classmate.

Do different blocks of wood with different densities float the same? Two compatriots investigate density by comparing the density of wood blocks with their floating levels. Each boy contributes to finding the answer. This simple experiment attracts their attention, demanding their complete awareness of the event.

CHAPTER 3

❖

Challenging Oneself

What are the real challenges children *should* face in their classrooms? Many would argue that they should master basic mathematical skills; learn strategies for mathematical problem solving; master spelling rules; understand and write in different genres; conduct fair-test science experiments; apply basic physics principles; and more. The list can go on for pages. Perhaps fresh and original challenges should be included.

One of my students attempts to build an electric motor. He is portraying Michael Faraday in our annual Sons and Daughters of the Galileo Society's History of Science Fair.

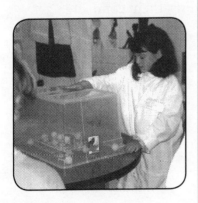

This student is illustrating a nuclear chain reaction using mousetraps and Ping-Pong balls. Her challenge was to learn to carefully set a trap by holding a Ping-Pong ball, covering the experiment, and dropping the last Ping-Pong ball into the closed transparent box. She portrayed Marie Curie.

A teacher can help his students reveal what they are capable of.

Each year we study weather, and students perform air pressure experiments for their friends. The children relish the "sense of mystery" found in these science demonstrations and applaud their classmates who share their accomplishments. Below, Cara demonstrates that placing a balloon in a jar and creating a partial vacuum results in the balloon's being inflated.

Above, Grady demonstrates a perpetual fountain using air pressure to force water out of one container and into another, resulting in a minifountain, to the delight of his classmates.

Below are photos of students demonstrating their perpetual fountains.

These three photos are of students instructing the class on the various adaptations of air pressure experiments.

Studying weather takes on a whole new meaning when students build their own instruments and test them at school.

Team building can develop a student's endurance and capacity to face new physical challenges.

For two seasons, another fifth-grade teacher, Nicole Doner, and I organized September Team Building for our classes. I did observe that before each physical trial students experienced a sense of reluctance followed by a hefty vitality. And after each accomplishment, there was an intense celebration of success, which brought students an enormous sense of pride.

Outdoor challenges provide a very different problem. Students need to use their strength, balance, and willpower to succeed in ropes course activities. Nicole Doner—fifth-grade teacher—and I would take our classes to a team-building outdoor education center in the fall. When our students faced risky yet safe physical challenges, mutual encouragement, trust, and cooperation became the glue that bound these children together, providing them with a sense of family.

Following each of our team-building field trips, the children changed. I observed new relationships. Some students took on new leadership roles and, with their new successes, found themselves more popular and better admired by their friends. Children who found classroom learning challenging discovered that they had unique talents and skills vital for success when they faced outdoor challenges. They found new respect and admiration from their peers, who now held them in higher esteem for their talents in organization, communication, and politeness.

I observed students encouraging and rooting for their friends, since team building required cooperation and support in order for the entire group to achieve success. Nicole and I would gather our classes, knowing full well the enormous benefits that would follow from these whole-day adventures.

He is the one and only.
He is the hawk waiting for you to show your work.
He is the lion using his strength and power to help you
learn more and more every day.
He is who he is: Mr. Puglisi.

—Keona Murray

CHAPTER 4

❖

Teamwork

Teamwork promotes genuine relationships among children; encourages students to depend on one another; furthers their capacity to cooperate and share ideas and strategies; and advances their emotional growth and development.

> When two or more students discuss different ways to solve problems, there are the beginnings of a creative dialogue, which is the root of inventiveness and a direct path to developing successful collaboration skills.

After a few weeks at school, my students became more and more proficient with teamwork. Learning together in close proximity became standard. This skill, however, needs to be closely monitored by the teacher, who gives feedback and talks with groups in need of guidance and suggestions. Teamwork was new for my students, because in previous years much of their learning was individualistic, not cooperative.

> Coming together is a beginning. Keeping together is progress. Working together is success.
>
> —Henry Ford

When we understand what children want from us, we can give it to them. They seek contact with each other, engaging in making new connections and exchanging ideas. Teamwork is a natural human impulse, and when it is implemented in the classroom, children *will* behave in a civil manner toward each other. There is diligence mixed with hilarity as these children indulge in the entire endeavor. What is gained in the end is a faith in oneself and in others. Fellowship, and colleagueship was the key to our success

Teamwork sometimes results in a *new creation*. Students designed math board games after a unit on numeration. Others used Hula-Hoops to illustrate various geometric attributes of the circle. Each coterie found its own nook—in the hall, at a table, or in the learning center. Their exuberance was evident in the chatter, laughter, and curiosity. Sometimes we educators misunderstand the value of children's chatter as a sign of discord, but in reality it is harmony speaking in different tones.

CHAPTER 5

❖

Total Focus

*You don't always have to rely on behavior modification or
special brain training.*

Touching up the RMS *Titanic*, reconstructing Mount Everest, weighing plants, and observing earthworms can all be sources of inspiration. Children can sustain long periods of concentration when they are challenged with using both their minds and their bodies. This approach is often called "hands-on" learning. Classroom noise level rises and diminishes as students are engaged in what captures their attention and interest. They can sustain themselves for quite some time. The top left photo shows one of my students adding touches to a model of the *Titanic*. He portrayed Robert Ballard in the World's Great Explorers Fair. The student in the above right photo is adding contour lines to a model of Mount Everest. He was Sir Edmund Hillary in our World's Great Explorers Fair.

When children are given projects and activities that require the use of the tactile sense, acute observation skills, device manipulation, and the recording of data, their attention spans extend beyond expectations. Weighing, observing, and measuring earthworms will hold children's attention for surprising long periods of time. My job becomes that of a facilitator who constantly monitors their behaviors and asks what they see, what they have discovered, and what they have recorded.

What we don't see is that children are mentally working through their own series of intricate calculations.

Total focus reaches deep into children's inner cores. Each becomes engrossed in the task at hand. At the conscious level, they carry out a mental dialogue of what to do next, correcting any slipups. Sometimes they carry on a monologue. At the subconscious level, a paradigm shift is taking place in the classroom. Students are now the directors. They are concentrating, focusing, thinking, listening, and paying attention to what they are doing. Sometimes I stand back and admire the enormous amount of talent each child has.

How can a small plant gain so much weight just by a person's giving it water on a regular basis?

CHAPTER 6

❖

Walking in Another's Footsteps

Here is what was asked of me. Here is what I have done.

The most challenging topics or units of study we had undertaken were those wherein my students adopted the personae of either great scientists or great explorers. After about six months in my classroom, they were ready to apply all of their creative and academic talents to these formidable tasks. The Sons and Daughters of the Galileo Society's History of Science Fair was the most challenging.

First I studied and prepared experiments for those scientists students selected. At any one time, about fifteen different experiments or activities took place. My partner, Debbie Richardson, and I transformed our rooms—one a laboratory, the other a place for writing biographies—into places to prepare PowerPoint presentations.

For about six weeks, students rehearsed their experiments. They prepared life-size murals of their scientists or explorers, as well as the types of costumes they would wear. One year, with the help of the art teacher, Karen Gitlin, students constructed marionettes of their explorers. The World's Great Explorers Fair lasted a full week in our library/media center, as the children entered an almost mythical life by portraying their chosen scientist or explorer. These children are the embodiment of tomorrow's future scientists and explorers.

A student portraying Leonardo Da Vinci.

A student portraying Sally Ride.

A student portraying Michael Faraday.

A student portraying Joseph Priestly.

How often do our children revel in their achievements?
What is in a child's mind when she portrays Sally Ride
or demonstrates a way to produce oxygen?

CHAPTER 7

❖

Celebrations

How often do students celebrate their achievements? Is there a paucity of these occasions in our schools? Is there any benefit to these forms of commemorations? The answer to this last question is, absolutely, yes. Children need to honor their accomplishments. These brief events build pride and a sense of unity. During these times, all are in accord and share each other's individual creativity. I ask myself, Can a single day in the life of these children be transformed into a dream for their future?

During my last three or four years of teaching, I discovered another way to enrich my classroom. It was called Habits of Mind. Habits of Mind founders are Art Costa and Bena Kallick. *"Habits of Mind are the characteristics of what intelligent people do when they are confronted with problems, the resolutions of which are not immediately apparent."* Art Costa.

Each week we studied one of the relevant Habits of Mind characteristics, and viewed various videos that illustrated Habits of Mind traits. One year we watched the video *Daniel and the Towers*. We agreed that each student would design his or her own tower at home and bring it to school. The photos above are a celebration of these students' creative talents. Appendix G list those Habits of Mind I introduced to my students.

CHAPTER 8

❖

Enjoying the Moment

I remember, neither with fondness nor with a sense of comfort, my elementary school days. There were no opportunities to laugh and celebrate or to express enjoyment, pleasure, or satisfaction. Perhaps it was these sad memories that would affect the way I taught children. We all need to *enjoy the moment*. The more often we find authentic experiences and freely express our joy, the more frequently learning becomes a constant celebration.

Children express their enjoyment in so many different ways. Each individual has his or her own personal way of expressing joy and pleasure. Living and learning in the company of children, I realized that, given the freedom to express themselves, children will spontaneously show their teacher those personal moments of joy.

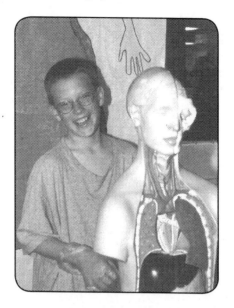

CHAPTER 9

❖

Sharing One's Knowledge

Students should have opportunities to demonstrate their knowledge by conveying what they have learned to their classmates and to adults. For many years, my students applied their time and talents to two very successful school-wide performances. For about five years, my students participated in the annual Sons and Daughters of the Galileo Society. Later, I initiated the World's Great Explorers. Students explained to teachers, parents, and classmates the history and contributions of scientists and explorers. These events lasted between three to five days in our library/media center. It took one full day to set up the projects and displays. Students visited for a full day, and parents were invited one evening. Appendices A and C include a list of these scientists and explorers.

Each year, someone wanted to be Albert Einstein. I had constructed a very large rotation platform and purchased a battery-operated train. Our young Einstein would rotate the platform both clockwise and counterclockwise while the train was stationary, moving forward, or going in reverse. Visitors began to witness that their perception of the moving or stationary train was dependent on the rotating platform as well as on the train. The train could be moving forward while the platform rotated backward, and the train could be perceived as being stationary.

CHAPTER 10

❖

Satisfaction Guaranteed

Given the opportunity, students willingly display their accomplishments. When children are able to express their achievements, it is like money deposited into their bank accounts. The investment pays off. They're ready for the next challenge.

As you view all of these photos, try to imagine the effort and time these children took in designing and completing their models of the Watts towers. What you don't see is all the writing, reading, and conversations between the children and me.

Euphoria is contagious when children display their individual creative talents.

Photos of students displaying models of their Watts towers.

The definition of *classroom* changes when children celebrate their creations. Perhaps in their minds the classroom becomes a temple or sanctuary where they can freely design and create without interference from or judgment by their teacher.

CHAPTER 11

❖

Reaching the Outer Limits

One year while learning about the Habits of Mind, we watched the video *Daniel and the Towers*. We recorded which Habits of Mind attributes could be observed. I proposed that groups build their own Watts towers. Our school custodian, Bob Gilman, volunteered to cut up two-by-four-foot and two-by-six-foot lumber into six-inch blocks. Students divided into teams and constructed their own Watts tower designs, and then they voted on the design they liked best.

The winning Watts tower model is shown in the left photo.

An opportunity appeared when several dozen empty computer boxes were piling up in the computer lab. I suggested to the children that we remove the boxes, paint them in the hall, and build a colossal Watts tower based on the winning wooden model—something never done before. For several weeks, we painted the boxes; then, we delivered them to the school stage; and one morning, we built our tower.

Students painting computer boxes for the Watts tower; photo on right.

Time passed—for most of us, several weeks elapsed. But for children who were "reaching the outer limits," time passed in a different way and could not be measured.

In children's minds, their personal Tree of Life is transformed into something rare, astounding, one of a kind.

The Watts tower designed and built by Horace Puglisi's fifth-grade class, 2008-09.

PART III

The Big-Picture Themes

CHAPTER 12

❖

Lessons of the Rain Forest

In 1997, I received a Christa McAuliffe Fellowship Award. With these funds, I traveled to Costa Rica with fellow educators and studied the tropical rain forest for two weeks. Returning to the classroom, I designed and implemented, with my partner Debbie Richardson, Lessons of the Rain Forest. The unit was fully integrated—it included science, social studies, and literacy.

The highlight of the unit was our weekly visits to the University of Vermont conservatory. There, Colleen Armstrong, greenhouse director, helped me design and implement a series of plant biology experiments. Ellie Morency, art teacher, assisted students with drawing these wonderful plant specimens. Debbie Richardson, having been offered a UVM classroom to teach in, instructed students in writing a variety of stories about rain-forest animals, plants, and environmental issues.

Two students take notes so as to describe their plants.

For six consecutive weeks we spent a full day at the UVM conservatory. Each student was given a plant to draw, observe, and record the physical attributes of. In two "houses," students carried out a variety of plant biology experiments.

Adding to the greenhouse experiments and drawings, Debbie Benoit (my partner) helped students create their own science and literature books, encouraged them to discover that there are ways to save the rain forest, and supervised the production and performance of a musical based on *The Great Kapok Tree* by Lynne Cherry. Rounding out the Lessons of the Rain Forest unit, students wrote original poetry and prose, and produced a bound rain-forest-themed book with a dedication, essays, poetry, stories, reports, glossaries, and information about each author. Below are a few samples of the children's writing.

Thoughts and Feelings about the Rainforest

In the rain forests of the world everything is connected, and every species depends on one another. It is important that we save the rain forest, because if we don't, the Earth's climate will change and many species will die. Some species might include the macaw, quetzal, jaguar, howler monkey, three-toed sloth, and, eventually humans.

Picture yourself in a steaming green, lush forest. It is the year 2000. You see animals like the quetzal, macaw, and sloth. All the levels of the forest are full of exotic life.

Now picture yourself in the same place, but in the year 2010. All you see is barren desert with smoldering trees and various bones scattered here and there. The sun is beating down, and it feels like a toaster oven!

This really could happen if the deforestation of the tropics continues. Every minute, sixty acres of rain forest are destroyed! Only the people who care can save the rain forest . . .

—Daniel Allen

Once I Dreamt

Once I dreamt I was the rain forest,
Full of beautiful and majestic life,
Full of shadows dancing through the parted leaves.
The water falls cool and clear.
Now you can see the beauty of me.

—Lauren Sheftic

Once I Dreamt I Was the Earth

Once I dreamt I was the Earth
My rain forests were in danger
Many people had cut them down
I know about species humans do not
People think it doesn't matter
Little do they know
I am getting polluted by the minute
People deserve to know
It's everyone's misfortune
The mahogany, the banana,
The cinnamon, the citrus
That's only a few of the many
Endangered plants in the rain forest

—Geoff Amey

Spirits

Spirits of the forests
Souls trying to find their way
Trapped in the forest

—Parvez Pathiawala

Macaws

Flying gracefully
Against the blue background sky
Rainbow of colors

Howler Monkeys

Swinging, tree to tree
Screeching about the forest
Duwoop! Ooo-ooo-ooo!

—Meredith Lee

Mr. Puglisi,
You are an owl in the classroom, hooting his way
through our minds.
A great oak making us climb to the top of our
potential.
A brainteaser, weaving our brains into cobwebs to
capture the information.
You are the roma tomato in the garden of learning.

—Jordan Meyer

CHAPTER 13

❖

Sons and Daughters of the
Galileo Society

*This is my absolute favorite unit of study,
and it is the most difficult.*

 Why would any
teacher have his students
study for a month and
then present a weeklong
fair on the history of
science? For five years,
beginning each April,
we prepared for a June
celebration of some of the
world's greatest scientists.
Appendix A is a partial list of those scientists students selected.

Using LinkWay, students reviewed all of the scientists. Groups included the Greeks, physicists, chemists, meteorologists, and biologists. Students chose three and then, with my help, finally selected their scientist. I met individually with each student, providing a packet of experiments their scientists had done. Then I set up a laboratory station for each student, gathered materials, and guided each student in his or her experiments.

In the adjacent room, Debbie Richardson coached students in writing their biographies. In the hall, other students drew and colored their huge murals of scientists. Often, two students teamed together to present on one scientist. In our classroom, students were conducting experiments in and creating projects about chemistry, physics, meteorology, paleontology, biology, and the Greek philosophers.

Andreas Vesalius presented
by two fifth-grade students.

Leonardo Da Vinci's *Mona Lisa*

Using a rotating platform under a swinging pendulum, a young Galileo illustrates how the earth (shown as a clock) rotates counterclockwise, causing time to move forward, or clockwise.

A young Michael Faraday teaching about electromagnetism.

The children learn firsthand a much bigger picture of science. Their classmates practice experiments in physics, chemistry, biology, and meteorology. Some prepare mineral displays, while others use scientific apparatuses such as a Van de Graaff generator, a helium laser, microscopes, a planetarium, and a Geiger counter.

He is the core that keeps us all together and
helps us reach toward our true limits.
He is the chalkboard that keeps and spreads
every detail it knows.
He is laughter, which keeps us joyful as we
work.
He is a spider.
And when others are in his nest,
He lassos them into learning.
He is a carousel, giving us every detail as the
year goes by.
He is a world of information that has no shape
or size.

—Isaac Kranz

CHAPTER 14

❖

World's Great Explorers

Thousands upon thousands of American children grow up on stories about Davy Crockett, Johnny Appleseed, Casey Jones, Daniel Boone, and Ethan Allen. Historically, many elementary students examine the early European explorers whose goals were to survey and gain control of New World lands. The traditional aim has been to identify the names of these individuals, their conquests, and their impact on the Western human environment. It was my dream that these children's heroes would be explorers such as Sir John Franklin, Matthew Henson, Mary Kinglsey, Thor Heyerdahl, and Amelia Earhart. Their studies reach much further back into the history of exploration and forward well into the twentieth century.

Why the World's Great Explorers unit? Because I wanted my students to understand the circumstances those explorers faced, as well as the challenges, risks, and discoveries they experienced, which have contributed to the history of exploration and discovery.

Below are some of the *big* ideas I wanted students to grasp as they learned about these explorers.

- What is necessary for any type of exploration to be successful?
- Are explorers heroes, villains, or both?
- Does exploration always lead to progress?
- Are there sets of universal qualities that are necessary to be a successful explorer?
- What drives explorers? Why do explorers subject themselves to such hardships?

While leading students in their discoveries in the World's Great Scientists unit, I began contemplating adding a new piece to this unit—the Six Facets of Understanding, based on the book *Understanding by Design: The Six Facets of Understanding* by Grant Wiggins and Jay McTighe, published by the Association for Curriculum and Development.

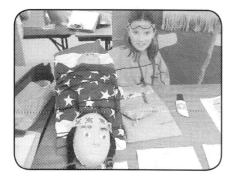

All students had to prepare a PowerPoint presentation about their explorer based on the Six Facets of Understanding. Below are those facets.

1. *Going Deeper/Providing Explanations*—What do you know? I want to know if your knowledge about your explorer goes beyond mere facts such as dates, travel routes, and names. Provide us with a full account of the main events of your explorer's adventure. How did your explorer plan and organize his or her adventure or voyage? What adversities

did your explore overcome, and what skills or qualities were needed?

Alexander the Great

2. *Interpretations*—Imagine that you have become your explorer's closest companion on the journey. How have you personally related to your explorer? What personal qualities can you share about this person? How did your explorer make his or her decisions? What are some qualities that set your explorer apart from other people you have known? Provide us with a powerful and complete picture of your explorer's personal qualities and traits.

3. *Applications*—Your task is to construct or build an explorer's mask that is an image of your explorer. Your mask should show us one of his or her personality traits, or perhaps portray your explorer in some type of situation you read about. Your mask should show us that you truly understand the importance of this artifact and have constructed a detailed representation of your explorer.

4. *Perspectives*—From your point of view, what is the value of learning about your explorer? Were the accomplishments worth the risks and dangers? Overall, did your explorer have a more positive or more negative impact on the places

and inhabitants he or she explored and encountered? If you were able to go back in time from the twenty-first century, reenter the entire experience, and advise your explorer, what suggestions and guidance would you give to that person?

5. *Empathy*—Explain how you have come to really appreciate and understand this person. What are the feelings and unusual qualities this person possesses? Explain that you not only understand the struggles your explorer encountered, but also that you understand how your explorer *felt* during his or her difficult times. Try to make us all really and truly understand this person and appreciate all of his or her qualities.

6. *Self-Knowledge*—What questions do you have about explorers in general? How much do you feel you understand about the qualities of an explorer? What misunderstandings do you have at this time? How does your explorer fit into the big picture of other great explorers? If you were to teach people to be explorers, what would be some of the main ideas of your instruction? What do you feel you don't understand about exploration, and what do you intend to do about it?

Sacagawea and her baby Pomp at one of our World's Great Explorers fairs.

CHAPTER 15

❖

The Columbus Voyage

While reading about Columbus' discovery of America and learning about his multiple voyages and hardships, we decided to hold a one-day, overnight simulation of the first voyage.

One year, students learned the names of Columbus' crew. Before their voyage, each received a blessing from Queen Isabella. That day, we set sail, and the entire crew spent the night in the Founders learning center. Parent volunteers arrived the next morning, offering breakfast to the young explorers.

CHAPTER 16

❖

Serving Others—Adding Quality to Our Lives

Learning must be experienced, so we studied life in the cafeteria kitchen.

Many of us are familiar with the many service organizations such as Rotary, UNICO, and Habitat for Humanity. Rotary Club members provide humanitarian service to community organizations. UNICO encourages high ethical standards in all vocations, and helps build goodwill and peace in the world. UNICO also promotes and enhances the image of Italian Americans. *Habitat for Humanity is a nonprofit ecumenical Christian ministry founded on the conviction that every man, woman, and child should have a decent, safe, and affordable place to live.*

I wanted my students to experience *serving others*. One year, I talked with our cafeteria manager, Lydia King, about having my students learn the food service operation—including ordering food, preparing meals, and serving students. She was enthusiastic and supported such a venture. For several weeks, groups of my students spent their mornings in the school kitchen learning about how food was ordered, seeing how lunch was prepared, applying math skills in calculating food orders, and discovering the rules regarding serving students. After about three weeks, our class planned a luncheon, selected which food to order, helped prepare and cook the school luncheon, and served students. Later, we discussed the experience. Comments were about how *good* the children felt about their service to other students; having fun in the kitchen, preparing and cooking food; learning something *not* in the classroom; and getting to know personally the cafeteria staff. All thought the whole experience was *fun*.

CHAPTER 17

❖

Peopling of America

One year, our class embarked on a course different from the traditional social studies curriculum. I wanted the children to learn about some of the great Americans who left behind important legacies that impacted our culture. For several weeks I searched the internet for the names of outstanding artists, journalists, musicians, poets, writers, philantropists, clergy, politicians, and more. History is about people and their unique contributions (in our case, to America). Children easily identify with historical figures, and I wondered if they would eagerly apply all their talents and skills in uncovering the lives of influential historical figures.

I discussed this with the children, who jumped at the idea. From a PowerPoint presentation illustrating these Americans, each child chose an American who had influenced our lives and culture. See Appendix H for a list of these Americans. After researching their chosen figure's life, each student prepared his or her own three—to five-minute-long PowerPoint presentation. When ready, the children, many in full costume, presented an assembly for the entire student body. One student who selected Louis Armstrong performed a trumpet solo.

With the PowerPoint presentations monitored by my good friend and colleague Paul Garrett, each student took turns standing on the stage and speaking to the entire student body. (Public speaking is one of many literacy skills in our curriculum.)

When the program was over, the entire student body was silent for several moments, and then huge applause erupted. I recall seeing several teachers teary-eyed.

CHAPTER 18

❖

Iqbal

As part of our literacy program, Afternoon Read-Aloud occurred each day after our recess and lunch break. I would read from a book for about twenty minutes, then use various techniques for eliciting student feedback. One day, a student brought a book titled *Iqbal* by Francesco D'Adamo and asked if I would read it to the class. I did. I could never predict the events that followed. *Iqbal* is a fictionalized account of the true story of a young boy who was sold into bonded labor in Pakistan. His family cannot afford to keep him at home. Chained to a carpet loom, Iqbal and other children are overworked and abused. One day, Iqbal manages to escape and is rescued by an aid agency. He travels to the United States and speaks publicly about the forced-labor conditions of children—bonded laborers. These are children whose labor is pledged by parents as payment on a debt.

Reading about being enslaved from a child's point of view struck deeply into my students' hearts and minds. All of us could feel *real pain. Was there any action we could take?* we wondered together. We learned that a young twelve-year-old, Craig Kieburger from Thornhill, Ontario, had learned about Iqbal Masih's tragic life, and as a result he formed the Save the Children Foundation.

In the teachers' room were dozens of boxes of used books left by teachers. I suggested to the children that we take all those boxes of books, arrange them on the school stage steps, and sell them. All of our money would be sent to the Save the Children Foundation. We all carried boxes to the stage, arranged books, and sold almost all of them. We then donated all of our profits to the Save the Children Foundation, which raises funds from pop sales, car washes, and bake sales run by children.

Iqbal
Masih
1982-1995

In 1995, Iqbal Masih was murdered after speaking out against slave labor.

PART IV

Special Events

CHAPTER 19

❖

Creative Ingenuity and Marshmallow Accelerators

How does a teacher take a fresh group of individual fifth graders who are beginning to get acquainted in September and begin teaching them that reading, writing, PVC tubing, and marshmallows are all connected? He brings to the classroom a collection of creative ingenuity books for students to read, and he surprises them with boxes of PVC pipes and connectors. The task is to build a simple marshmallow accelerator, and the teacher tells the students that they can work alone or in small groups and build their own.

When the children had assembled their accelerators, we marched past classrooms and gathered outside to test our devices by shooting mini-marshmallows. Students tested their accelerators for the longest and most accurate flight. It was a wonderful way to begin the year. The next day, we discussed what made this event so successful.

Later, I introduced students to their first writing genre—the procedural essay. Their task was to list their materials and write down the procedure they used to build their marshmallow accelerators. With the help of Paul Garrett, we used a software program to draw each individual accelerator.

One year, I had students write about the value of creative ingenuity. Below is one student essay.

Are Creative Experiences in School a Good Thing to Have?

Have you had any creative experiences in school? Do you think creative ingenuity should be taught in schools? This year in Mr. Puglisi's class, I had the opportunity to expand my creative talents. I made a marshmallow accelerator and a Watts tower, I transformed an egg carton, and I created a sandwich.

I think it is terrific to be given a chance to be creative in school. I learned that I have the talent to design unusual things. I made a marshmallow accelerator out of PVC pipes, made a Watts tower out of wooden blocks, and transformed an egg carton into a change organizer.

Some people think that creative ingenuity is a waste of time and doesn't teach you anything. They argue that we should focus on math facts, reading, science, and history. However, there are other skills that are helpful and important to have. These skills are being more flexible, being able to design useful things, and being an individual. These lessons taught me that I am unique and have special creative abilities. Let's look at some reasons why creative ingenuity is a good skill.

The first reason I support creativity is because it showed me that I have creative skills I did not know I had before. Besides that, some jobs involve creating things, and if there was no creativity, lots of people would lose their jobs. We might not have cars or telephones without creative ingenuity. Another reason I support creative ingenuity is because we would not have many of the things we currently have. In conclusion, creative ingenuity is a helpful and useful skill to have.

—Sarah Thompson

CHAPTER 20

❖

Morning Meetings and Poems by Jack Prolanski

Each morning, at around 6:45 a.m., I would begin my one-hour commute from Randolph to Essex. I had plenty of time to think about the school day, the children, and which lessons needed to be reviewed. I would pilot my car into its usual parking spot and notice the same cars in their normal places. We're creatures of habit. Some mornings I paused outside and observed the children running and scampering out of their school buses, crashing into the school's front door—only to be reminded of our code of conduct. They filed into the gymnasium and patiently waited for dismissal.

It's 7:50 a.m., I approach my classroom. A classroom without children is like an empty cavity, silent, with no energy and no vitality. But in moment, the landscape will change. A few minutes pass, and the entire second floor is resurrected by the surge of children. The hallways, once quiet and empty, are now full of young hearts beating, keeping pace with hurried footsteps. Some children burst into the classroom, drop their backpacks, and hurry to renew yesterday's friendships. Small groups congregate and socialize. Some students begin using a computer to finish or continue their writing assignment. Still others show friends what they will share during the morning meeting. Others stroll directly to the coat rack, carefully unpack, and amble to their desks. On the screen is the morning message, which highlights those tasks that will begin the day, as the children navigate around their classroom.

Our morning meeting begins around 8:35, when I signal the class with a chime. They gather on the carpeted area. One side has a long, two-by-ten-foot bench supported by cement blocks. In front are two low lab tables. Students gather around, some sitting on the bench, others kneeling around the double table, others sitting on chairs. Some always seem to sit in close proximity each morning. Others are satisfied filling any available space. The area is carpeted with a Home Depot rug—not a Persian, but suitable. The children find their niche awaiting the promise of new stories or items to see. Sharing time is *not* a brief interlude separating attendance taking and the morning meeting from learning. It is a productive segment of each day where a "circle of love" offers a bounty of good feelings to begin the day. It is a time when *all* of us acquire the habits of human decency. By my modeling listening to each student's story, encouraging others to share or "piggyback" on a friend's comments, and supporting those who remain quiet, the children learn each morning new ways to respect and value their classmates. Mondays are the best. The children are again reunited—reconnected. Many of the children eagerly await their friends to give a full account of their weekend exploits. Some children share their experiences; others talk about their dreams. Some bring items to share. A few will be satisfied just to listen to their friends. Occasionally, a child will share stories that clearly identify some feelings of loneliness or discouragement.

What stories will they divulge this morning? We are all here making ourselves at home. Will today be a world of order and harmony? I look for any outward manifestations that may betray hidden feelings and thoughts. A few weeks into the new school year, our classroom is now a place where some of the children feel rescued, resurrected by their friendships and the love they share. I must remember to offer compliments after their stories, giving confidence to the whole class. Is there a child carrying any sorrows from yesterday or joys from the bus ride? I scan the group to see if there is anyone who might be angry, disappointed, or aloof from the group. Will I have any words of wisdom during our morning meeting?

These sharing times began a "new life" each morning. Children learned the habits and characteristics of their friends.

Idiosyncrasies or peculiarities of some of them were at first ignored, and later anticipated, as students began to look forward to the stories of their friends.

I began reading poems written by Jack Prolanski. The children loved these humorous stories, and Mr. Prolanski's poems became a tradition. One morning I read the poem "Sandwich Sam." And at the end I asked if the students would like to schedule a sandwich-off. A sandwich-off is a sandwich competition. Students voted to have a sandwich-off the next week, and we all agreed to a number of categories; "most nutritious," "most attractive," and "most original" were three of them. Another event was the Great Cookie-Off.

Our cafeteria director, Bonnie Zarkowski, helped judge the varied cookie recipes.

During the sandwich-off event, I tasted all of the students' sandwiches and posed with Hannah, one of my students, for this photo.

CHAPTER 21

❖

Halloween Madness

Why not celebrate Halloween as a classroom learning experience? Each year I encouraged my students to bring to class all of the candies they collected the night before. No one objected. For almost a week, we applied a variety of math skills as we studied our candy. We calculated the total amount of

candy collected. We found the mean, median, and mode of certain candies. We determined the most popular candy.

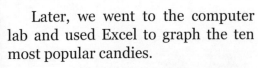

Later, we went to the computer lab and used Excel to graph the ten most popular candies.

For the children, it was one week of pure mathematical fun. As teachers, we normally seek a state of equilibrium—where events are often predictable and controllable. Halloween Madness and Marshmallow Accelerators may appear to be oddities within the traditional scheme of things. However, these types of events offer the children an opportunity to learn, act, and behave in a state of disequilibrium. During Halloween Madness, not everyone has the same candies or the same number of candies. The classroom has a new fragrance and is alive with children sharing their various treasures. We discover that learning can become a continually changing state—advancing and developing. The children, who discover that Halloween is lot more than trick-or-treat, are advancing and developing as well.

PART V

Curriculum Connections

CHAPTER 22

❖

The Habits of Mind

Following the success of the science and explorer fairs, which introduced the Six Facets of Understanding to the children, I began searching for a way to reach all my students throughout the year. "Facets" only worked very well with my most competent, conceptually oriented students, who were able to apply all six facets to the study of their explorers. Habits of Mind appeared to be just what I was looking for.

Emeritus Professor Arthur L. Costa of California State University at Sacramento is the author of *Habits of Mind*. He identifies sixteen traits, or characteristics, that intelligent people apply when facing challenging problems. These are not ways of thinking but, rather, behaviors that can be adopted by anyone. Would my students adopt some or all of these qualities? And how would I educate them to do this? Appendix G lists the Habits of Mind.

I made an effort to introduce a new Habit of Mind every other week. Simply talking about the trait was insufficient. I needed to identify examples for these children. I discussed my plans with our library media director, Judy Kaplan, and searched for videos that offered evidence of Habits of Mind. Watching the videos and having students check for what they believed to be examples of Habits of Mind proved to be very successful. The movies that students were most engaged with and found many relevant examples in included *Fly Away Home* and *The Polar Express*.

With these visual images, the children were able to identify Habits of Mind during morning meetings when we discussed one of the selected Habits of Mind and shared how we applied that characteristic at school and at home. Those Habits of

Mind that the students most often were able to identify as part of their behaviors were persistence; managing impulsivity; listening with empathy and understanding; thinking flexibly; and thinking interdependently.

Persistence was the most identifiable trait. The students were able to easily identify circumstances where they showed increasing persistence. Persistence is defined as *sticking to it; persevering in a task through to its completion; remaining focused; looking for ways to reach your goal when stuck; not giving up.*

Managing impulsivity was new for the students. I don't believe schooling helped students understand how to remain calm and thoughtful. With the help of videos and morning meeting discussions, the students became more and more aware of situations that triggered impulsive behaviors, and they learned how to manage these behaviors. Managing impulsivity is defined as *thinking before acting; remaining calm, thoughtful, and deliberative.*

Listening with empathy and understanding required more time and discussion. I don't believe schools encourage this behavior among children. Schools are too often focused on passing on knowledge to children rather than on helping them. This trait is evidenced by *understanding others; devoting mental energy to another person's thoughts and ideas; making an effort to perceive another's point of view and emotions.*

Thinking flexibly requires both teacher and student to have intellectual relationships. Intellectual conversations help children *look at it another way; become able to change perspectives, generate alternatives, and consider options.* Conversations with students in our reading groups offered this opportunity. Rather than looking for "right" or "wrong" answers, we asked for varied opinions, interpretations, and insights to help students think flexibly.

Thinking interdependently had been the prevalent classroom modus operando. Including this behavior as a classroom goal and *learning from others in reciprocal situations and through teamwork* became discussion topics at our morning meetings.

William Glasser, American Psychiatrist, has clearly stated that: at "the heart of all good education, where the teacher asks students to think and engages them in encouraging dialogues, constantly checking for understanding and growth."[1]

---

[1]

CHAPTER 23

❖

Mathematics for All Students

Mathematics for All Students was designed to challenge the most gifted of my math students yet also provide a comprehensive program for those needing much more assistance. The children studied mathematics each morning for at least one hour, beginning around 9:00 a.m., after morning meeting. There were three components to my math program—whole-group presentations, group contracts, and word problems. Our geometry unit was organized much differently.

The Math Program

The whole-group presentations were organized around four themes: numeration, computation, operations, and rational numbers. Within each theme, there were about twenty contracts, with four to eight pages per contract. I organized and prepared the four themes. No textbooks were used. Using transparencies and my overhead projector, I presented topics to the entire class. After about twenty minutes or so, the class broke into groups and began solving the math contracts. Students who needed assistance with either the presentation or their math contracts would meet with me. Students were free to choose their partners. Usually, they formed groups based on ability. Students who were very proficient often chose to work together. Less capable students banded together and often met with me for assistance. I learned an important lesson—I would frequently observe a student sitting or kneeling, not writing, sometimes appearing unfocused. I would ask, "What are you doing?", and the response I would get would be, "I'm thinking."

After about a month, I introduced the word problems, which are presented in Appendix B. Many of the challenging problems were taken from a MENSA calendar, and many were quite difficult. On Mondays, I introduced the word problem, and students were given one week to solve it. Each time I proposed a new word problem, some students had puzzled expressions, and others appeared totally baffled. The following Monday, students volunteered to present their solutions to the class using the overhead projector. My purpose was *not* to encourage only my most proficient students, but to allow anyone who was willing to share his or her solution to do so. After several weeks, the more reticent students discovered that I was more interested in their thinking than in whether or not their solutions were correct. I scored the word problems using the following criteria: approach and reasoning; connections; solution; math language; math representation; and documentation.

Geometry

Geometry became our most popular mathematics topic. Students who were skillful in computations and mathematical reasoning were challenged with pentominoes and tangrams. Others were very skillful when we visited the computer lab and applied Microsoft Logo to constructing geometric shapes. I included a number of geometry contracts requiring lots of spatial challenges. The most difficult geometry topic was the polyhedron. I had several dozen small wooden polyhedrons. Students had to compute the volume of these polyhedrons and clearly show their solutions.

While studying geometry, students used Hula-Hoops to illustrate geometry concepts such as radius, chord, central angle, and tangent.

Pie "Pi" Day

Each year, we measured the diameter and circumference of different-sized circular wooden discs. The children discovered that no matter the size of the circular disc, the ratio of diameter and circumference was constant. Their calculations always resulted in a value close to 3.1415. The lesson didn't end with this discovery. We celebrated our accomplishments with Pie "Pi" Day. Students brought homemade pies to school. We measured the diameter and circumference of each student's pie. Again, our results were close to 3.1415. Then we celebrated by feasting on all of the homemade pies.

He is the happy in a gloomy day.
He is a penguin diving to find knowledge and
learning something new every day.
He is the wise owl who guides us through different
roads in life.
He is the seed in our mind,
Helping us bloom by showering us with
information.
I am the sunflower, he is the sun.
I am looking up at him for his advice and
knowledge.
He is always willing to try something new,
Even if it involves risks.
We are so lucky to have him.
I bet everyone else who had him would say the
same things.

—Elise Carnery

Chapter 24

Literacy

After about six years teaming with my partner, Debbie Richardson—she using her skills in writing and reading while I continued teaching math and science—our fifth-grade classes experienced a decline in population. We now needed not six but five classrooms. I was selected for a solo teaching experience. Knowing full well that solitary and singlehanded teaching has its disadvantages, I began a new teaching relationship with an extremely competent educator—Kathy Grace. With collegial support from this special educator and expert in spelling, I applied the many complex spelling rules to the various topics students were learning.

Concerning my desire to organize reading into varied themes, I turned to Judy Kaplan, media director. She introduced me to the rich selection of the Dorothy Canfield Fisher Award books. Studying the many topics and accompanying books, she and I built a thematic approach to reading. Appendix D lists all of the books I read and introduced to my students.

Reading was usually scheduled in the afternoons. Reading groups were formed for each theme, and children often conferred with me about their selections. Contracts were written for specific books. A generic contract is illustrated in Appendix E. Appendix F contains a specific book contract.

My intention for our afternoon literacy program was to assist and encourage my students to develop multifaceted approaches to reading. I had to find ways to enhance my students' intellectual processes as they gained meaning from the words they read. I chose books so that students would be able to decode and understand meaning in context and so they could gain a deep understanding of the text they were reading.

The hidden-message theme was "a hope for better things." What this means is that completing one book could lead to the ability to gain insight into an author's literary style as well as the complex relationships among the characters. My plan was for each child to find success in the words, phrases, paragraphs, and chapters. With each success, reading was no longer "work requiring overcoming a resistance." It became work with dignity. Pride and self-esteem were the rewards.

Afternoon Read-Aloud

Children love stories, especially if the speaker changes his pitch, inflections, and cadence. While completing my doctoral residency at the University of Connecticut, I took a course in storytelling. I listened to about a dozen elite storytellers and carefully noted not only their stories but also those facets that made their stories attention-grabbing and appealing. Two storytellers I listened to and learned from were Jay O'Callahan and Tim Jennings.

I began with humorous stories such as *The Giant Hogstock* and *The Finches' Fabulous Furnace* and ended with books such as *A Single Shard*.

The art of storytelling is primarily the skill of keeping the audience's attention. But more importantly, I employed think-aloud strategies daily. I would pause and ask if anyone had a personal experience or knowledge related to what I was reading. My intent was to evaluate how much of the story might be relevant to the children. Quite often I would stop and ask for predictions about what might happen next. My interest was to assess what reactions they were having to the story. Occasionally, I would pause and ask what mental pictures the children had of the story setting, or what so-and-so looked like. I would give students opportunities to ask questions so I could understand which students might be confused and which appeared to be probing for a deeper understanding. Depending on the story, I might inquire as to which items or parts of the story they were "packing away" that helped them make sense of the story as it unfolded. A question I always remind myself to ask was, "What does this story mean to you?"

Whiz Kids' Vocabulary

Beginning in October or early November, the children were given five difficult vocabulary words on each Monday. They had five days to find the meanings and learn how each word was divided into syllables. At first, the children were astonished by these vocabulary words. I told them that neither their dictionaries nor the library dictionaries would help at all. Their only resource was the Internet. In the beginning weeks, about half of the students found the meanings. After a month, the entire class was eager for the next set of vocabulary words. I had personally selected all of these words from several books which listed words for the "Superior Person." Each Friday, students were scored on correct meaning, correct syllabication, and neatness. After several weeks eighteen or nineteen out of twenty three students received perfect scores. The children delighted in discovering words such as *dirhinous, ergasiphobia, defenestration, discombobulate, alopecia, acerebral,* and *confabulate.*

Appendix I lists these words in the typical order they were given to the children.

Etymology and Greek Roots

In the mid-1990s I had just completed an etymology class at the University of Vermont. The district was beginning to include an introduction to Greek and Latin roots. One of our resource literacy books included a list of root words. Rather than use these words only in late spring, I regularly presented my students with a wide-ranging list of nouns, adjectives, and verbs that I had learned in class. Each word was broken into its basic Latin or Greek parts. The children were fascinated by how our common words had been constructed. Each was given his or her own Latin/Greek journal to keep and find useful in the future. Appendix J includes a selected list of words students learned.

Fiddling Around

There is no doubt of the need for increased literacy—reading and writing. Perhaps the time-tested method for improved reading is to give students more experience with writing. Fifth-grade students are introduced to and expected to show proficiency in a variety of writing genres. During my last seven or eight years of teaching, I worked closely with Kathy Grace, who is considered an expert in literacy and conducts workshops throughout Vermont and New England. Our collaboration proved very successful. But something was missing—A Celebration in Writing.

In the winter of 2006, I introduced the staff to a PowerPoint on the Fiddlehead Project. It was a comprehensive way to offer systemic change in instruction. Included was a *Fiddlehead Periodical* comprised of students' stories, poems, and art. The goal was to encourage more creative thinkers in our school population by having students write. The staff adopted the periodical idea, and several classes sent their students' writing to be included in our published journal. Appendix K includes examples of students' "Fiddling-Around Stories."

CHAPTER 25

❖

The Magic of Science

How do you present science so that many of the experiment results appear magical? When children experience magical events that are either thrilling or unpredictable, then that occurrence becomes locked in their memories for many years. Below are some examples of experiments that became enduring components in our science program.

The Incredibly Shrinking Marshmallow Man

Using a vacuum chamber and vacuum pump I purchased, students learned firsthand the properties of an environment devoid of air pressure. What happens to a marshmallow man or a cup of warm water when all the air pressure around each is eliminated? Each year during our weather unit, I took out our vacuum chamber, assembled marshmallows in the shape of a marshmallow man, and placed him in the vacuum chamber. The children, wearing safety goggles, gathered around in a tight circle. After I asked for predictions about the fate of our marshmallow man when all of the air was removed, the children predicted that "nothing would happen, he would shrink really small." To their astonishment, our marshmallow man expanded and tripled in size. After witnessing several trials, they began to clearly explain the cause of his phenomenal growth. When air was allowed to reenter the vacuum chamber, our marshmallow man shriveled into a tiny, wrinkled old man.

When I placed a cup of water in the vacuum chamber and asked for predictions about what would happen when the air was removed, my students were astonished to witness the water boiling after a few minutes when the vacuum pump was running. They all believed that the water got really hot, because it was boiling. But when a few carefully placed a finger in the cup of water, they were surprised to find that the water was at room temperature. They began to learn the physics behind the boiling of water.

Keeping Up with Free Fall

What happens when an object falls to the ground? The great Italian physicist, mathematician, astronomer, and philosopher Galileo Galilei (1564-1642) asked the same question. During the time we studied the history of science, I introduced the children to Galileo. I purchased twelve—and fifteen-foot moldings to serve as ramps. Using metal spheres, we set up inclined planes and measured the distance the spheres traveled each second by using a stopwatch. The children discovered that the spheres accelerated with time. As we increased the slope, the spheres traveled faster and farther each second. I then posed the question: "How much does an object accelerate during its free fall?" These fifth graders needed more than learning about the free-fall formula or knowing that objects fall at a rate of ten meters per second. They needed to experience free fall while I explained to them that at one second, the object was falling at ten meters per second; at two seconds, that same object was falling at twenty meters per second; and at three seconds, that object was falling at thirty meters per second.

Using chalk and a meter measuring tape, I marked out on the blacktop the distance an object would reach at free fall each second. The first mark indicated zero meters. The second line indicated five meters; the third, twenty meters; and the third, forty-four meters. A fourth line showed seventy-eight meters. I explained that after one second, the free-falling object would have traveled five meters. At two seconds, the object would have reached thirty meters, and at three seconds, the object would have reached forty-four meters. I did explain that the object only reached these distances if there was no air or friction to slow its rate of speed. Next, the children took turns to see if their running could accelerate at a free-fall rate. No one could approach the two-second mark.

Life without Friction

With an understanding of Galileo's discovery of free fall, we needed to understand life without friction. With Chapter 2 grant funds, I purchased a high-quality air track. Experimenting with the air-track carts, the children discovered that objects move at a constant speed in a frictionless environment. The air track was a classroom fixture for several weeks. Children freely explored how carts accelerated as we angled the air track, learning how gravity affects acceleration.

Polymer Power

Children have firsthand experiences of or have heard of celluloid, cellulose, plastics, polyurethane foam, urethane, and leather. However, how many have had opportunities to make their own polymers? While studying chemistry, the most popular activity was the polymer experiment. The children made Silly Putty, foam, monster flesh, rubber, and other polymers.

Why learn about polymers? First of all, children lean basic chemistry techniques using apparatuses such as graduated cylinders, balances, and other glassware. They learn that there is an "order" to adding chemicals, and there are also important safety procedures. These experiments gave them firsthand experience in learning about the nature of physical properties. And they learned that chemical names had origins in the Greek language. *Poly*—is a Greek prefix meaning *many,* and *mere* is another Greek root, meaning *parts.*

Children enjoy handling rubbery objects like Silly Putty that can bounce easily. They made and handled sticky and gooey and stretchy polymers. Polymer study shows students that molecules can be made up of long chains of atoms linked together. Using small Styrofoam balls, we made long carbon chains, as well as simple molecules such as water, salt, sugar, and alcohol. Appendix M lists our polymer experiments.

Founders Woods

Founders Woods is part of our school campus. Founders Woods became our second classroom. To begin, I explored the woods and marked several "nature" trails. I noted trees, shrubs, groundcover, and ferns, and prepared a list of these plants. Included were their Latin names. The children spent hours in the woods. Being out in fresh air, exercising their bodies, learning in an outdoor environment, and discovering the variety of trees and the differences among ferns made for an extremely successful learning adventure. Students who were challenged in reading could easily identify various plant species. Those who had difficulty sitting quietly in a classroom found that the freedom of being outdoors, in the woods, was an entirely different and comfortable way to learn. The children acquired the ability to identify about twenty-four plant species, collected and pressed plants for their own leaf collections, and prepared scale maps of the woods. Appendix N lists those plants we studied.

The Greenhouse and Outdoor Classroom

During my fifth year of teaching at Founders, I conceived of a new and very challenging idea—A Greener World. Our superintendent, Ray Proulx, challenged teachers to propose new projects that could be funded through state and federal grants. The idea of designing a new component to add to our science program took root. I called it A Greener World. I devoted weeks to preparing the proposal, and I composed a forty-five-page funding proposal, which was mailed to dozens of funding agencies. Even though several found my proposal worthwhile, none were able to provide funding at the level I had requested. I turned to local fund-raising. In three years, I raised over $35,000 through the sale of T-shirts and annual plants, including my $6,000 NSF Science Teaching Award and funds from my Christa McAuliffe Fellowship. With assistance from the National Gardening Association, I designed and prepared a PowerPoint presentation showing how an unused plot of land adjacent to our school could be transformed into an outdoor classroom. Included was a forty-foot-long greenhouse, a potting shed, and raised gardens. With help from a group of enthusiastic parents, I presented the proposal to our school board, which approved the project. One year later, we had an outdoor classroom with a greenhouse, raised beds, and a potting shed. That year I was awarded the Vermont National Education Association's Teacher of the Year Award.

During the remaining years of my teaching career, my students had an additional outdoor classroom. In the spring, we raked fallen leaves that had covered the outdoor classroom grounds; cleared debris from the raised gardens; removed GrowLabs from the greenhouse; swept the floors; and cleaned shelves to make the greenhouse ready. We planted dozens of vegetable seeds in the GrowLab flats, and each May we held our annual plant sale.

PART VI

Closing Comments

CHAPTER 26

❖

The Classroom as an Oasis

In the beginning of this narrative, I wrote that one essential reason children come to school is to seek out friendship. I observed these happenings every fall as children entered our classroom. Most were happy and thrilled to see their old friends in the same class. Others, who saw no friends, were far less elated. When it came time to "buddy up" for their first projects, old friends bonded, while other students stood by watching.

Time and events will change the needs, wants, and desires of children. The classroom culture will transform. Beliefs and values the children once held evolve into a far more sophisticated system. I call this new structure the "Classroom as an Oasis." When children seek a definition of *oasis,* they find that the dictionaries state, "a place that provides refreshing relief." Another definition: "pleasant change from what is usual, perhaps annoying, and difficult." Probably one of the most sought-after oases for children and families is Disney World. Other people would choose the islands of Santorini and Kauai or cities such as Venice, Be'er Sheva, Jerusalem, Mecca, Angkor Wat, and Varanasi as an oasis.

The Classroom as an Oasis draws children's attention away from their own personal needs, wants, and desires. Imperceptible changes occur each day. Children enter the classroom, drop their backpacks, and pick up where they left off yesterday. Some hurry to a computer to continue their writing or look up a vocabulary word. Others check and feed our fish; small groups assemble and solve math problems in their math contracts. Several students check and water plants. A few find a comfortable place and read. Those who bring items to share or who take the time to fashion their own costumes find themselves surrounded by curious onlookers.

Learning doesn't begin at a prescribed time. No one waits for morning announcements. There isn't any distinction between work and play. As weeks turn to months, the children's heritage is on display. In a sense, they are emancipated from the original mental and emotional baggage or constraints that were dragging them down during the early weeks of school. Our time passes in its own way, and no one is counting. Often we're surprised that it's time for recess or that the day is over. On "good days," learning is contagious—teacher helping children, children helping children.

CHAPTER 27

❖

Cloudy and Rain Days

You're probably wondering if what I have written is genuine. All you have read is accurate. The photos are authentic and are included to offer a vivid and lasting impression of our classroom life. I made no effort to overdramatize my relationship with children. However, the story tries to illustrate the numerous examples of children's "rising to the challenge." Our classroom landscape was often intimate and personal, seldom competitive or adversarial.

However, the road from September to June can be bumpy. There are potholes and dead ends, and the weather can be chaotic. I faced a few thunderstorms. Quite often I was assigned students with lots of hidden potential who had yet to find success at school. I was assigned students with serious learning problems that had yet to be solved. And, students with persistent discipline problems found their way into my classroom. Occasionally I would have two students one of whom was a "Siamese shadow" of the other. No matter where or when one of these children would move, the other would follow. There seemed to be an *unspoken code* between them. Sporadically, a child would arrive in class and silently express all those things he or she would not allow him—or herself to share. The child would drop his or her backpack and jacket on the floor and meander about the room, finally settling at his or her desk, not paying attention to anyone. I wondered about what tangled thoughts were going on in that child's mind. Several times each year, a bond between two students would rupture. Perhaps jealousy arose, or one betrayed the other. The two would shun each other for a day or two, and then by some invisible force the two would be friends again.

Were there moments when I had taken time to reprimand a student? Yes. But let me be clear. There was no chastisement nor any admonishment. If I had taken to scolding, there would have been *no* growth within me. The reprimanded child could mentally downshift, feeling remorse or blame, perhaps anger. We would quietly enter the hall and have a quiet, brief conversation. I learned early in my teaching career that using my position as a way to intimidate, or "talk tough," would only serve to alienate a child. I also understood that I did not have a clairvoyant understanding of what was in any child's mind. Instead, the brief conversation would focus on describing the mischievous or unruly behavior, with a follow-up illustrating how those actions had a negative influence on the class. I would seek a commitment for change, shake hands with the student, and return to the class. As that child's behavior showed improvement, I would casually offer a quiet personal comment—"I like what you're doing." Perhaps these uncommon incidents left invisible yet vital imprints on my teaching.

There were moments when a student's outburst led me to call for help from one of our school counselors—Katie or David. The students who had gotten upset would not reveal whatever it was they were hiding. There was almost a denial and rejection of what the classroom would offer. There were days when other students came to class upset because they lost their best friend or believed no one liked them. Was there a magic formula for these challenges? Absolutely *not!* But there are solutions.

One successful remedy—given enough time—was that I would seek an easy flow between me and a troubled child. If he or she perceived an openness, a transparency of my own identity, then that child would begin to see me as I really was—another individual with the same feelings and needs; a teacher who offered an open door for a student to reveal his or her own gifts and talents; a teacher who would provide a hands-on learning environment. As time progressed, the student's wariness would diminish, and imperceptible changes in psychological alertness would take place. The student would join the class's Tree of Knowledge.

You recall the fable "The Princess and the Pea" by Hans Christian Andersen. "The Princess on the Pea" is a fairy tale about a young woman whose royal identity is established by a test of her physical sensitivity. The tale was first published with three others by Andersen in an inexpensive booklet on 8 May 1835 in Copenhagen by C.A. Reitzel. A young prince could not find a real princess; all those he had found had something wrong with them. During a heavy rain, a princess is allowed into the castle by the prince's father. But the prince's mother, the queen, is suspicious of the young girl. That night, she lays a pea on the bedstead and covers it with piles of mattresses, upon which the young princess is invited to sleep. The next morning they ask how she slept. Her reply is as follows:

"Oh, terribly bad!" said the princess. "I have hardly closed my eyes the whole night! Heaven knows what was in the bed. I seemed to be lying upon some hard thing, and my whole body is black-and-blue this morning. It is terrible!"

Almost each year I had one or two students who were unable to sit quietly or comfortably in their seats. They would squirm, wiggle, and sometimes fall off their chairs. I found several science lab tables and had the legs cut off of them so that students could kneel and use them. Any student who found it awkward or uncomfortable sitting at a chair could find comfort using these tables. The remedy worked!

What was I seeking? I wanted a group of children who had a contagious and infectious curiosity, and a desire to challenge themselves with tasks they would have never thought possible. I wanted these children to develop a proclivity—an appetite for new facts and attention to detail. My most important goal was to offer each child an opportunity to aspire to become something greater than themselves. I'm reminded of all of the great scientists and explorers my students studied. Below is a photo of one student who portrayed the famous and exceptional female explorer Amelia Earhart.

CHAPTER 28

❖

A Model for Teaching, Instructing, and Educating

Over my forty-six-year career in education, I gradually became aware that a guiding principle emerged as my overarching goal. Beyond the varied instructional techniques I continually added to my teaching toolkit and the ever-increasing teaching resources that filled my classroom and storage facilities. *I discovered that the essence of teaching is a Celebration of Children's Talents, which is a direct pathway to cohesiveness and interdependence in a classroom where friendship, family, and community are the norm.* Below is a simple paradigm illustrating this teaching model.

> A Celebration of Children's Talents—A Pathway to Cohesiveness and Interdependence for Friendship, Family, and Community

↑   ↑

> ## Classroom Themes and Topics
>
> Watts Tower, Sons and Daughters of the Galileo Society, Lessons of the Rain Forest, Morning Meetings, MENSA Word Problems, Halloween Madness, Marshmallow Accelerators, Math Journals, Math Contracts, World's Great Explorers, the Fiddling-Around *Fiddlehead Periodical,* Founders Woods Nature Trail, the Outdoor Classroom and Greenhouse, Mousetrap Cars, Catapults, Immigration, and more.

Curriculum Mandates	Teaching Resources

CHAPTER 29

❖

Some Thoughts, Advice, and Guidance

Passing on information . . .

As teachers of children, we are often compelled to pass on information, assuming that what we say is fully absorbed and becomes part of a child's mental framework, making him or her ready for action. But this seldom happens. Simply passing on information to a student who does not have in his or her own memory bank a similar experience means that the information only sits in his or her mind and is disconnected from experience.

Focusing Naturally

In our nature walks in Founders Woods as well as during the numerous field studies, my students could easily focus naturally because their minds were interested in what they were seeing. They were not asked to focus by staring or thinking hard about what they observed. When their focus was relaxed, not tense—as was too often the case in the classroom—these children were irresistibly drawn to whatever attracted their attention.

Losing Our Concentration

I recall clearly those many instances in teaching when I was dissatisfied with the moment. My mind would take me into what I believed to be the future, or into the past days and weeks in the classroom. Occasionally I became dissatisfied with what was taking place in the classroom. Sometimes we desire that our classroom be different from what it really is, and so we are pulled into an unreal world and are unable to appreciate what our children are doing and learning. We leave the reality of the present and prefer the unreality of past events or even future moments in time. If my teaching is taken over by desires for the future or influenced by past issues, then I am taken over by conflicting desires and I lose that precious moment of the here and now before me.

The Real Meaning of Self-Worth

How many of us recall our students returning to the classroom after recess? How many of them, both boys and girls, were caught up in the belief that their self-esteem was tied into how well they excelled in the sport they were playing that day? Sometimes how well they performed became a "life-and-death" drama. Some really believed that by being the fastest runner, the most accurate kickball player, or the superlative soccer player, they would be eligible for the recognition they wanted from their peers. Do our schools foster this belief? Or do parents bear the responsibility for it? Should we allow our children to measure their self-worth according to their abilities and achievements? If these children are driven by a compulsion to succeed, and if they assume that this will lead them to higher levels of happiness and self-respect, then they may ignore many other virtues, such as accountability, creativity, curiosity, diligence, and fortitude.

We live in an achievement-oriented society where people are measured by their competence in various endeavors. However, when we teachers observe our students caught up in win-lose situations, it is our responsibility to use these events as lessons during classroom meetings, helping our children understand that there are many ways to achieve pride and dignity. *And, most important, they learn from us that they are good people worthy of respect whether or not they do things successfully.*

Appendices

Appendices

APPENDIX A

Partial List of Sons and Daughters of the Galileo Society Scientists

Mary Ann Mantell

Robert Ballard

Claudius Galen

Albert Einstein

Charles Darwin

Gregor Mendel

Theodoric of Freiburg

Nicholas of Cusa

Virginia Apgar

Andreas Vesalius

Isaac Newton

Ernest Rutherford

Richard Feynman

Stephen Hawking

Benjamin Franklin

Ignaz Semmelweis

Thomas Graham

Alexander Graham Bell

Alessandro Volta

Johannes Kepler

Marie Curie

Tor Bergeron

Van de Graaff

Anna Botsford Comstock

Hippocrates

Rachel Carson

Louis Agassiz

Georgius Agricola

Joseph Priestley

Carolus Linnaeus

Thomas Edison

Theodore Maiman

Galileo Galilei

Tycho Brahe

Otto von Guericke

Aristotle

Leonardo Da Vinci

Ellen Marsden, University of Vermont

Archimedes

Charles Goodyear

Richard Feynman

Michael Faraday

Anton van Leeuwenhoek

Henry Cavendish

APPENDIX B

❖

Advanced Word Problems

Which is larger, 9/16 or 8/12?

(Include your Approach and Reasoning, Connections, Solution, Math Language, Math Representation, and Documentation.) You may use additional paper or the back side.

Which is larger, 5/7 or 0.7?

(Include your Approach and Reasoning, Connections, Solution, Math Language, Math Representation, and Documentation.) You may use additional paper or the back side.

If ¾ of a cup of sugar is enough for baking ⅔ of a cake, then how much sugar is needed to bake two cakes?

(Include your Approach and Reasoning, Connections, Solution, Math Language, Math Representation, and Documentation.) You may use additional paper or the back side.

It takes you five minutes to assemble a widget. One employer will pay you 50¢ for each widget you assemble. Another employer will pay you $7.00 per hour as long as you keep assembling widgets. Which employer would you rather work for?

(Include your Approach and Reasoning, Connections, Solution, Math Language, Math Representation, and Documentation.) You may use additional paper or the back side.

One brand of blank audiocassettes costs $4.79 for a pack of four. Another brand comes in a pack of six for $8.99 with a

$2.00 rebate slip. The stamp needed to mail the rebate slip costs 33¢. Which is the better deal?

(Include your Approach and Reasoning, Connections, Solution, Math Language, Math Representation, and Documentation.) You may use additional paper or the back side.

A car started a trip of 300 miles with a full tank of gas. The size of the tank is 12 gallons. The car used 7 gallons of gas to travel 161 miles. Will the driver be able to complete the trip without stopping to buy more fuel?

(Include your Approach and Reasoning, Connections, Solution, Math Language, Math Representation, and Documentation.) You may use additional paper or the back side.

A mathematician's will stated that his wife should get ⅓ of his estate; his son, 1/5; his older daughter, 1/6; and his younger daughter, $9,000.

Who received more, his older daughter or his younger daughter?

(Include your Approach and Reasoning, Connections, Solution, Math Language, Math Representation, and Documentation.) You may use additional paper or the back side.

In the multiplication puzzle below, x, y, and z represent different digits. What is the product of x, y, and z?

yx
z
zxx

(Include your Approach and Reasoning, Connections, Solution, Math Language, Math Representation and Documentation.) You may use additional paper or the back side

A fee of $2,000 is to be divided among five band members so that each gets $100 more than the next-younger band member. How much will the youngest band member receive?

(Include your Approach and Reasoning, Connections, Solution, Math Language, Math Representation, and Documentation.) You may use additional paper or the back side.

Three one-dollar bills were exchanged for a certain number of nickels and the same number of dimes. How many nickels were there?

(Include your Approach and Reasoning, Connections, Solution, Math Language, Math Representation, and Documentation.) You may use additional paper or the back side.

Let's say twenty-six zips weigh as much as four crids and two wobs. Also, eight zips and two crids have the same weight as two wobs. How many zips does it take to equal the weight of one wob?

(Include your Approach and Reasoning, Connections, Solution, Math Language, Math Representation, and Documentation.) You may use additional paper or the back side.

Can you position four squares of equal size in such a way that you end up with five squares of equal size?

(Include your Approach and Reasoning, Connections, Solution, Math Language, Math Representation, and Documentation.) You may use additional paper or the back side.

Suppose all the counting numbers were arranged in columns as shown below. Under which letter would the number 100 appear?

A	B	C	D	E	F	G
1	2	3	4	5	6	7
8	9	10	11	12	13	14
15	16	17	__	__	__	__

(Include your Approach and Reasoning, Connections, Solution, Math Language, Math Representation, and Documentation.) You may use additional paper or the back side

In the puzzle below, the numbers in the second row are determined by the relationships of the numbers in the first row. Likewise, the numbers in the third row are determined by the relationships of the numbers in the second row. Can you determine the relationships and find the missing number?

89	53	17	45	98
	25	16	17	26
	14	?	16	

(Include your Approach and Reasoning, Connections, Solution, Math Language, Math Representation, and Documentation.) You may use additional paper or the back side.

Can you determine the next letter in the following series?

A   C   F   H   K   M   ?

(Include your Approach and Reasoning, Connections, Solution, Math Language, Math Representation, and Documentation.) You may use additional paper or the back side.

There are six chairs, each of a different color. In how many different ways can these six chairs be arranged in a straight line?

(Include your Approach and Reasoning, Connections, Solution, Math Language, Math Representation, and Documentation.) You may use additional paper or the back side.

A man spent ¾ of his money and then lost ¾ of the remainder. He has $6.00 left. How much money did he start with?

(Include your Approach and Reasoning, Connections, Solution, Math Language, Math Representation, and Documentation.) You may use additional paper or the back side.

Nancy and Audrey set out to cover a certain distance by foot. Nancy walks half the distance and runs half the distance, but Audrey walks half the time and runs half the time. Nancy and Audrey walk and run at the same rate. Who will reach the destination first, or will it be a tie?

(Include your Approach and Reasoning, Connections, Solution, Math Language, Math Representation, and Documentation.) You may use additional paper or the back side.

Which is greater, 107 percent of 300, or 50 percent of 600?

(Include your Approach and Reasoning, Connections, Solution, Math Language, Math Representation, and Documentation.) You may use additional paper or the back side.

There is a certain logic shared by the following four groups of numbers. Can you determine the missing number in the last group?

1	13	17
18	-3	9
28	12	36
15	44	?

(Include your Approach and Reasoning, Connections, Solution, Math Language, Math Representation, and Documentation.) You may use additional paper or the back side.

Alex, Ryan, and Diane are sports fans. Each has a different favorite sport among football, baseball, and basketball. Alex does not like basketball; Steven does not like basketball or baseball. Name each person's favorite sport.

(Include your Approach and Reasoning, Connections, Solution, Math Language, Math Representation, and Documentation.) You may use additional paper or the back side.

I recently returned from a trip. Today is Friday. I returned four days before the day after the day before tomorrow. On which day did I return?

(Include your Approach and Reasoning, Connections, Solution, Math Language, Math Representation, and Documentation.) You may use additional paper or the back side.

If ½ of 24 were 8, what would ⅓ of 18 be?

(Include your Approach and Reasoning, Connections, Solution, Math Language, Math Representation, and Documentation.) You may use additional paper or the back side

The two numbers together have the same relationship to each other as the other two number pairs. What is the relationship, and what is the missing number?

3, 8   -5, 24   0, 1   9, 80   4, 15   6, ?

(Include your Approach and Reasoning, Connections, Solution, Math Language, Math Representation, and Documentation.) You may use additional paper or the back side.

What is 10 percent of 90 percent of 80 percent?

(Include your Approach and Reasoning, Connections, Solution, Math Language, Math Representation, and Documentation.) You may use additional paper or the back side.

What is ½ of ⅔ of 3/5 of 240 divided by ½?

(Include your Approach and Reasoning, Connections, Solution, Math Language, Math Representation, and Documentation.) You may use additional paper or the back side.

What single-digit number should go in the space where the question mark is?

6	5	9	2	7
1	4	3	5	?
8	0	2	8	1

(Include your Approach and Reasoning, Connections, Solution, Math Language, Math Representation, and Documentation.) You may use additional paper or the back side.

If the ratio of 5x to 4y is 7 to 8, what is the ratio of 10x to 14y?

(Include your Approach and Reasoning, Connections, Solution, Math Language, Math Representation, and Documentation.) You may use additional paper or the back side.

Ten boys and eight girls can shovel as much snow in twelve days as eight boys and twelve girls can shovel in ten days. Who are the faster workers, the boys or girls, and by how much?

(Include your Approach and Reasoning, Connections, Solution, Math Language, Math Representation, and Documentation.) You may use additional paper or the back side.

What is the missing number in the following series?

13   7   18   10   5   ?   9   1   12   6

(Include your Approach and Reasoning, Connections, Solution, Math Language, Math Representation, and Documentation.) You may use additional paper or the back side.

What is the value of the following?

$$\frac{1}{3 + \frac{1}{3\frac{1}{3}}}$$

(Include your Approach and Reasoning, Connections, Solution, Math Language, Math Representation, and Documentation.) You may use additional paper or the back side.

When purchased together, a pair of binoculars and the case cost $100. If the binoculars cost $90 more than the case, how much does the case cost?

(Include your Approach and Reasoning, Connections, Solution, Math Language, Math Representation, and Documentation.) You may use additional paper or the back side.

Suppose a, b, and c represent three positive whole numbers. If a + b = 13, and b + c = 22, and a + c = 19, what is the value of c?

(Include your Approach and Reasoning, Connections, Solution, Math Language, Math Representation, and Documentation.) You may use additional paper or the back side.

Find the missing number in the following series.

5/12   ⅓   ¼   1/6   1/12   ?

(Include your Approach and Reasoning, Connections, Solution, Math Language, Math Representation, and Documentation.) You may use additional paper or the back side.

A box of chocolates can be divided equally among three, six, and eleven students. What is the smallest number of chocolates the box can contain?

(Include your Approach and Reasoning, Connections, Solution, Math Language, Math Representation, and Documentation.) You may use additional paper or the back side.

What are the two missing numbers in the series below?

8   15   10   13   12   11   14   9   17   7   ?   ?

(Include your Approach and Reasoning, Connections, Solution, Math Language, Math Representation, and Documentation.) You may use additional paper or the back side.

What is the value of z in the following problem?

```
  x
  y
+ z
 xy
```

(Include your Approach and Reasoning, Connections, Solution, Math Language, Math Representation, and Documentation.) You may use additional paper or the back side.

How many digits must be changed in the following addition problem to make the sum equal 245?

```
  89
  16
+98
```

(Include your Approach and Reasoning, Connections, Solution, Math Language, Math Representation, and Documentation.) You may use additional paper or the back side.

A cube measuring four inches on each side is painted blue all over and is then sliced into one-inch cubes. How many of the smaller cubes are painted on three sides?

(Include your Approach and Reasoning, Connections, Solution, Math Language, Math Representation, and Documentation.) You may use additional paper or the back side.

Here's an interesting twist on an old series puzzle. See if you can come up with the missing letter. (Hint: This problem is best approached with an even hand.)

T   F   S   E   T   T   F   ?

(Include your Approach and Reasoning, Connections, Solution, Math Language, Math Representation, and Documentation.) You may use additional paper or the back side.

Twice a certain number is fifteen less than five times the same number. What is that number?

(Include your Approach and Reasoning, Connections, Solution, Math Language, Math Representation, and Documentation.) You may use additional paper or the back side.

One number is larger than another by seven, and their sum is thirty-three. What are these numbers?

(Include your Approach and Reasoning, Connections, Solution, Math Language, Math Representation, and Documentation.) You may use additional paper or the back side.

A grocery store sells a certain cereal in two sizes: 12 ounces for $1.29, or 18 ounces for $1.79. Which is the better deal?

(Include your Approach and Reasoning, Connections, Solution, Math Language, Math Representation, and Documentation.) You may use additional paper or the back side.

One store has a certain item on a "buy two, get one free" sale. The store across the street is selling the same item at 30 percent off the normal price. Which is the better deal?

(Include your Approach and Reasoning, Connections, Solution, Math Language, Math Representation, and Documentation.) You may use additional paper or the back side.

Machine A produces 150 widgets in forty minutes. Machine B produces 500 widgets in two hours. Which machine is faster?

(Include your Approach and Reasoning, Connections, Solution, Math Language, Math Representation, and Documentation.) You may use additional paper or the back side.

A slow airplane leaves at 8:00 a.m. on a flight to a city 720 miles away. It flies at 180 miles per hour. A faster plane, one that flies at 480 miles per hour, is flying from the same airport to the same city, but it will not depart until 10:45 a.m. Which plane will get you there earlier?

(Include your Approach and Reasoning, Connections, Solution, Math Language, Math Representation, and Documentation.) You may use additional paper or the back side.

APPENDIX C

❖

List of the World's Great Explorers

Some of the world's great explorers chosen by students are listed below. I documented each explorer's life and achievements so that each student would have an idea of this information beforehand. I made an extensive library collection, including videos, available for students. As part of this study, students created a PowerPoint presentation about their explorer, organized around the Six Facets of Understanding.

1. Alexander the Great—334 BC; most outstanding Greek explorer
2. Amundsen, Roald—20th century; first to reach South Pole
3. Anker, Conrad—20th century
4. Armstrong, Neil—20th century; first person to set foot on the moon
5. Baker, Ian—21st-century explorer of Tibet's Tsangpo Gorge
6. Ballard, Robert—20th-century American undersea explorer
7. Bass, George—20th century; discoverer of the oldest shipwreck known
8. Battuta, Ibn—1325; traveled from Morocco to China
9. Bebee, William—designed the bathysphere with Otis Barton
10. Bingham, Hiram—discoverer of Machu Picchu, Lost City of Incas
11. Byrd, Richard—flew over South Pole in 1929
12. Cabot, John—18th-century Italian explorer who sailed to Canadian provinces
13. Cabot, Sebastian—18th century; explored South American coast
14. Carter, Howard—opened the tomb of Tutankhamen
15. Cartier, Jacques—18th century; explored St. Lawrence River

16. Cavelier, René-Robert, Sieur de LaSalle— French explorer who led the first expedition to track the Mississippi River, ca. 1669
17. Clark, William—19th century; led expedition across Rocky Mountains to Pacific Ocean with Meriwether Lewis
18. Columbus, Christopher—discoverer of New World
19. Cook, James—18th-century explorer who mapped New Zealand and the east coast of Australia
20. Cousteau, Jacques—20th century; inventor of the aqualung
21. Da Gama, Vasco—18th century; first European to reach India by sea
22. Darwin, Charles—19th-century British explorer of South America and Galapagos Islands
23. De Balboa, Vasco Núñez—16th century; explored Isthmus of Panama, sighted Pacific Ocean
24. De Champlain, Samuel—16th-century French explorer
25. De Soto, Hernando—16th century; reached Mississippi River, explored present-day southeastern United States
26. Drake, Sir Francis—first Englishman to sail around the world, 1577
27. Earhart, Amelia—20th-century aeronautics explorer
28. Earle, Sylvia—21st-century deep-sea explorer
29. Eric the Red—982, sailed to Greenland from Iceland
30. Flinders, Matthew—circumnavigated Australia
31. Fossey, Dian—20th-century gorilla explorer
32. Franklin, Sir John—19th-century polar explorer
33. Frobisher, Martin—English explorer of Hudson Bay
34. Goodall, Jane—20th century foremost expert on chimpanzees
35. Hawass, Zahi—21st-century Egyptian archeological-explorer
36. Hawkins, Heidi—21st-century high-altitude explorer
37. Hedin, Sven Anders—Swedish explorer of China and Tibet
38. Hensen, Matthew—1909, member of first expedition to reach North Pole
39. Heyerdahl, Thor—20th-century Norwegian who sailed the Kon-Tiki raft from Peru to Polynesia

40. Hillary, Sir Edmund—20th century; first European to climb Mount Everest

41. Ho, Cheng—15th-century Chinese maritime explorer who reached as far as Africa

42. Hudson, Henry—17th century; explored Hudson Bay and Hudson River

43. Kinglsey, Mary—1893, explored West Africa

44. Leakey, Louis—20th century; paleoanthropologist

45. Lewis, Meriwether—19th-century American explorer

46. Livingston, David—19th century; greatest European explorer of Africa

47. Magellan, Ferdinand—16th century; commanded the first voyage around the world, 1519

48. Ötzi the Iceman—Neolithic traveler found in the northern mountains in Italy

49. Peary, Robert—led first expedition to reach North Pole, 1909

50. Polo, Marco—1271, visited central Asia, China, Sumatra, Ceylon, India, and Persia

51. Ponce de León, Juan—17th century; explored Florida

52. Ride, Sally—first female American astronaut to explore space; orbited earth for seven days

53. Rock, Joseph—20th century; explored China and Tibet; anthropologist and botanist

54. Sacagawea—Shoshoni woman who acted as a guide and interpreter for Lewis and Clark

55. Sereno, Paul—20th-century paleontologist

56. Shackleton, Ernest—20th-century Irish explorer of the South Pole

57. Stanley, Sir Henry—19th century; found source of Nile River, explored the Congo River

58. Steeger, Will—20th-century Arctic explorer

59. Sterling, Matthew—20th century; discovered pre-Colombian Mexican civilization

60. Tereshkova, Valentina—Russian, first woman to travel in space

61. Vespucci, Amerigo—16th century; made several voyages to the West Indies and South America

Appendix D

❖

Theme Books

With the assistance of our library's media director, Judy Kaplan, I included a wide range of reading material for students. The year was divided into themes. The first was Creative Ingenuity. Books were assigned based on the reading abilities of the students. One of my responsibilities was to have read every book assigned or selected by students. Also, I prepared reading contracts for many of the books. Students were able to work in small groups and answer the questions.

Creative Ingenuity

Gadget War
Chalk Box Kid
The Not-Just-Anybody Family
Frindle
Butch and Spike
Seedfolks

Conflict

Boy at War
The Art of Keeping Cool
Waiting for Anya

Against All Odds

Level 6 and Above
It's Nothing to a Mountain
Hatchet
Among the Hidden
Just Juice
The Black Bonnet

Dear Austin
I Thought My Soul Would Rise and Fly
The Last Safe House
I Rode a Horse of Milk White Jade
Among the Hidden
Island of the Blue Dolphins
Railway Children
Homecoming
Anne Frank: The Diary of a Young Girl
Rosa Parks
Shadow of the Bull
A Single Shard
Out of the Dust
Esperanza Rising
Through My Eyes
The Watsons Go to Birmingham
The Year of Miss Agnes
Sidewalk Story
Saving Lilly

Level 5

When My Name Was Keoko
Dragonwings
Shadow Spinner
Kite Fighters
Crispin: The Cross of Lead
Through My Eyes
Holes
Runaway Children
The Shakespeare Stealer

Levels 4-5

Sahara Special
Monkey Island
Whipping Boy
Louisiana Sky
Ella Enchanted
Midwife Apprentice
Out of the Dust
Bud, Not Buddy
Saving Lilly
Good Night, Maman
Sarah Special
Homeless Bird
Joey Pigza Loses Control

Levels 3-4

Stone Fox
The Canada Geese Quilt
Day of the Blizzard
Patrol
Hunt
Secret of the Seal
The Big Wave
Whipping Boy

What Jamie Saw

Coming of Age

A Step from Heaven
Hoot
Tangerine
I Rode a Horse of Milk White
Jade
Surviving the Applewhites
The Great Turkey Walk
Walk Two Moons
Joey Pigza Loses Control
A Single Shard
The Shakespeare Stealer
Bat 6
The Big Wave
Shadow Spinner
The Year of Miss Agnes
The Spray-Paint Mystery
Just Juice
Power of Un
Because of Winn-Dixie
Scorpions
The House of the Scorpion
The House on the Gulf

Journeys

I Rode a Horse of Milk White
Jade
The Giver
Holes
Running Out of Time
Dragonwings
Esperanza Rising
The Watsons Go to Birmingham
The Big Wave

Wanted Dead or Alive: The True
Story of Harriet Tubman

Only Connect

Holes
A View from Saturday
The Thief
Bat 6
Out of the Dust
Free-Form Verse

Other Times, Other Places

Crispin: The Cross of Lead
Running Out of Time
Among the Hidden
A Single Shard
Pictures of Hollis Woods
When My Name Was Keoko
Shadow Spinner
Tuck Everlasting

Survival

Hatchet
The Voyage of the Frog
The Young Man and the Sea
Where the Lilies Bloom
Island of the Blue Dolphins
Winter Camp
Joey Pigza Loses Control
Today's Families
Who Am I?

Political Revolutions

The Fighting Ground

Sarah Bishop
War Comes to Willy Freeman
My Brother Sam Is Dead
The Winter of Red Snow

Colonial America

A Journey to the New World:
The Diary of Remember
Patience Whipple
The Discovery of the Americas

Slavery

Dear Austin
The Black Bonnet
The Last Safe House
I Thought My Soul Would Rise
and Fly

Explorers

Over the Top of the World
Thor Heyerdahl and the
Kon-Tiki Voyage
The Incredible Journey of
Explorers Lewis and Clark
Captain Cook
Where Do You Think You're
Going,
Christopher Columbus?
The Journal of Augustus
Pelletier
First Women of the Skies
The Voyage of Columbus
Against All Opposition—Black
Explorers in
America

Richard E. Byrd
Adventures to the Poles
Jacques Cousteau
Robert Ballard
Ice Story
Pedro's Journal
Remarkable Voyages of Captain
Cook
Night of the Twister
Weather

Unusual Creatures

The Tale of Despereaux
Ella Enchanted

Coloring Outside the Lines

Hoot
A Step from Heaven

Personal Narrative

The Shakespeare Stealer
Saving Lilly
Crash
Keeper of the Doves
What Jamie Saw
Belle Prater's Boy
Shadow of a Bull
Monkey Island
The View from Saturday
Shadow Spinner
Where the Lilies Bloom

Biography

At Her Majesty's Request

Red Scarf Girl
Mary on Horseback
Ethan Allen
Rosa Parks: My Story
Wanted Dead or Alive: The
True
Story of Harriet Tubman
Walking the Road to Freedom:
A Story about Sojourner Truth
True Confessions of Charlotte
Doyle
Anne Frank: The Diary of a
Young Girl

Stories Read to the Class

The Giant Hogstock
The Finches' Fabulous Furnace
Because of Winn-Dixie
Shadow Spinner
A Single Shard
I Rode a Horse of Milk White
Jade

Question-Answer-
Response-
Based Books

Earthquake
The Year of the Panda
20,000 Leagues Under the Sea
Silver
Danger Guys
Staying Nine
Shoeshine Girl
Earthquake

Appendix E

APPENDIX E

❖

Generic Reading Contract

Book title:_____

Author: _____

Student's name: _____

Date started: _____

1. **Vocabulary**—List several interesting words you discovered in the story. Please be ready to explain why you chose these words.

   _____
   _____

   What is the setting of the story?

   _____

   Who is the narrator?

   _____

   Is or was the narrator a real person or a fictitious person?

   _____

   Write about the main character. What kind of person is he or she?

   _____
   _____
   _____

How much time passes after the opening episode? Does time jump around or unroll evenly? Does time pass slowly?

_____
_____
_____
_____

What are the important changes in the story?

_____
_____
_____
_____

2. **Retelling the story**—Retelling is a brief review of most or all of a story, including several major events. The retelling gives the reader a sense of the events. Below is a frame you can use to write a story retelling:

This story is about _____
who _____. It takes place in _____. In this story, the problem starts when _____. After that, _____.
Next, _____. Then, the story ends with _____
_____.

3. **Summarizing the story**—Summarizing is different from retelling.

The most important ideas are _____.

The story takes place in _____.

The main characters are _____.

The main problem of the story is _____.

Key events from the story are:

_____

_____

_____

_____

The outcome or resolution of the problem is (when)

_____.

(Leave out unnecessary information and details.)

4. Metacognitive Awareness

Check at least one statement to explain what you did to help you understand this story.

( ) I recalled what I knew about this topic.
( ) I asked myself questions as I read.
( ) I decided what was important to remember.
( ) I could picture what was happening.
( ) I was reminded about similar books and experiences.
( ) I used the textual cues or features in the story to help me
   decide what was important.

Explain below one of these strategies you used to helped you understand what you were reading.

_____

_____

_____

_____

5. Connection Questions

When did you become very curious about what you were reading?

_____

List some of the pages where you made connections between this book and another book. Name that other book.

_____

List some of the pages where you made some type of meaningful connection between what you were reading and your own life. Please be ready to explain why.

_____

List some of the pages where you made a connection between what you were reading and events that have taken place in the United States or another country.

_____

APPENDIX F

❖

Esperanza Rising **Reading Contract**

Book title: *Esperanza Rising*
Genre: Against All Odds
Author: Pam Muñoz Ryan

1. **Phonics**—Below is a list of vocabulary words taken from *Esperanza Rising*. Find five words that fit under each of the following categories. Remember that syllable types are controlled by their vowel patterns, so pay close attention to the vowel(s) and the combination(s) within the words. Use the description of each syllable type, which should be in your binder, to help you.

Words that Have Closed Syllables	Words that Have Open Syllables	Words that Have Silent *e* Syllables	Words that have r-controlled Syllables	Words that Have Suffixes
1.	1.	1.	1.	1.
2.	2.	2.	2.	2.
3.	3.	3.	3.	3.
4.	4.	4.	4.	4.
5.	5.	5.	5.	5.

2. **Vocabulary**—"I found interesting words in this story. They are listed below, along with the page number where they can be found." Choose five to ten words and build a word pyramid for your words. For example, "I've chosen 'capricious'—a high-powered word. It means 'whimsical,

erratic, impulsive, and unpredictable.'" *Ask for the word pyramid sheet.*

Premonition—p. 9

Capricious—p. 13

Mesmerized—p. 64

Monotonous—p. 72

Untethered—p. 92

Nauseous—p. 92

Staccato—p. 93

Contagious—p. 156

Repatriation—p. 170

Pneumonia—p. 182

Susceptible—p. 183

"Dirty greasers"—p. 188

Indignation—p. 188

Voluntary deportation—p. 207

Novena—p. 214

Skeptically—p. 248

Esperanza—p. 26

4. **Parts of Speech**—Choose sixteen words from the above list to add to the chart below. You should have four words for each category.

Noun (a person, place, or thing)	Verb (an action word; something you can do, like run, walk, etc.)	Adjective (a word that describes a noun)	Adverb (a word that describes a verb, indicating how an action is done; it usually ends in the suffix—*ly*)

What is the setting of the story?

_____

Who is the narrator?

_____

Write about the main character. What kind of person is he or she?

_____

_____

_____

How much time passes after the opening episode? Does time jump around or unroll evenly? Does time pass slowly?

_____

_____

_____

What are the important changes in the story?

_____

_____

_____

5. **Retelling the story**—Retelling is a brief review of most or all of a story, including several major events. The retelling gives the reader a sense of the events. Below is a frame you can use to write a story retelling:

This   story   is   about   _____
who   _____. It   takes   place   in
_____. In this story, the problem starts when
_____. After that _____.
Next, _____. Then, the story ends with _____
_____.

6. **Summarizing the story**—Summarizing is different from retelling.

The most important ideas are _____.

The story takes place in _____.

The main characters are _____.

The main problem of the story is _____.

Key events from the story are _____.

The outcome or resolution of the problem is (when) _____
_____.

(Leave out unnecessary information and details.)

7. **Literal Comprehension Questions**

8. **Interpretation Questions**

9. **Reflection Questions**

The main characters in this story are Esperanza, Mama, Abuelita, Miguel, Isabel, and Hortensia. Do any of these characters remind you of yourself or acquaintances in real life? Please explain.

_____

_____

In this story, the author includes the expression, "Wait a little while and the fruit will fall into your hand." What does this expression have to do with the story?

_____

_____

On page 14, Abuelita explains to Esperanza, "There is no rose without thorns." What is Abuelita's hidden message?

_____

_____

Do you agree with Abuelita that when you drink tea from rose hips, you take all the beauty that the plant had possessed? Whether you do or do not agree, what is Abuelita trying to tell Esperanza (page 35)?

_____

_____

Explain in your own words what the title of the story means to you. And, does the title relate to the story?

_____

_____

Imagine if you were Esperanza. How would you react to the death of your father, life in the work camp, and your mother's illness? Would anything be easy for you?

_____

_____

10. Metacognitive Awareness

Check at least one statement to tell what you did to help you understand this story.

( ) I recalled what I knew about this topic.
( ) I asked myself questions as I read.
( ) I decided what was important to remember.
( ) I could picture what was happening.
( ) I was reminded about similar books and experiences.

( ) I used the textual cues or features in the story to help me decide what was important.

Explain below how you used one of these strategies to help you understand what you were reading.

_____

_____

_____

_____

_____

APPENDIX G

❖

Habits of Mind

Persistence

Stick to it! Persevering in a task through to its completion; remaining focused. Looking for ways to reach your goal when stuck. Not giving up.

Managing Impulsivity

Take your time! Think before acting; remain calm, thoughtful, and deliberative.

Listening with Empathy and Understanding

Understand others! Devote mental energy to another person's thoughts and ideas; make an effort to perceive another's point of view and emotions.

Thinking Flexibly

Look at it another way! Be able to change perspectives, generate alternatives, and consider options.

Thinking about Your Thinking: Metacognition

Know your knowing! Be aware of your own thoughts, strategies, feelings, and actions, and their effects on others.

Striving for Accuracy

Check it again! Always do your best. Set high standards. Check and find ways to improve constantly.

Applying Past Knowledge

Use what you learn! Access prior knowledge; transfer knowledge beyond the situation in which it was learned.

Questioning and Posing Problems

How do you know? Have a questioning attitude; know what data are needed, and develop questioning strategies to produce those data. Find problems to solve.

Thinking and Communicating with Clarity and Precision

Be clear! Strive for accurate communication in both written and oral form; avoid overgeneralizations, distortions, deletions, and exaggerations.

Gathering Data through All the Senses

Use your natural pathways! Pay attention to the world around you. Gather data through all the senses—taste, touch, smell, hearing, and sight.

Creating, Imagining, and Innovating

Try a different way! Generate new and novel ideas, fluency, and originality.

Responding with Wonderment and Awe

Have fun figuring it out! Find the world awesome and mysterious, and be intrigued by phenomena and beauty. Be passionate.

Taking Responsible Risks

Venture out! Be adventuresome; live on the edge of your competence. Try new things constantly.

Finding Humor

Laugh a little! Find the whimsical, incongruous, and unexpected. Be able to laugh at yourself.

Thinking Interdependently

Work together! Be able to work with and learn from others in reciprocal situations. Use teamwork.

Remaining Open to Continuous Learning

Learn from experiences! Have humility and pride when admitting you don't know; resist complacency.

❖

The Peopling of America

Aaron Copland
Aldo Leopold
An Wang
Anne Hutchinson
Ansel Adams
Antonia Novello
Benjamin Franklin
Bill Cosby
Booker T. Washington
Captain John Smith
Cesar Chavez
Chief Joseph
Chief Red Cloud
Chief Sitting Bull
Clara Barton
Connie Chung
Dorothea Dix
Dorothea Lange
Edward Flanagan
Edward R. Morrow
Eleanor Roosevelt
Eli Lilly
Faith Ringgold
Fiorello LaGuardia
Frederick Douglass
George Catlin
George Gershwin

George Wythe
Harriet Beecher Stowe
Harriet Tubman
Henry Wadsworth Longfellow
Hillary Rodham Clinton
Irving Berlin
Isaac Asimov
Jackie Robinson
Jacob Riis
Jane Addams
John James Audubon
John Steinbeck
John White
Julian Bond
Katharine Lee Bates
Louis Armstrong
Louisa May Alcott
Margaret Mitchell
Marian Anderson
Marian Wright Edelman
Marjory Stoneman Douglas
Martin Luther King
Mary Cassatt
Maya Angelou

Myra Colby Bradwell
Olaudah Equiano
Pearl Buck
Pete Seeger
Ralph Waldo Emerson
Reverend Cotton Mather
Richard Rogers
Rosa Parks
Ruth Bader Ginsburg
Samuel Francis Smith
Samuel Gompers
Sandra Day O'Connor
Sojourner Truth
Saint Frances Xavier Cabrini, Virgin
Stephen Foster
Susan B. Anthony
W.E.B. Du Bois
Walter Cronkite
William Bradford
William Penn
Woody Guthrie
Yo-Yo Ma

APPENDIX I

❖

Vocabulary Words

Dirhinous	Nullibiety	Xenopus
Bimanal	Persnickety	Indubitable
Grallatorial	Bumptious	Sudatorium
Defenestration	Carpe diem	Piscatorial
Kakistocracy	Bugaboo	Paludicolous
Kindergraph	Ochlophobia	Melliferous
Abecedarian	Haplography	Sitology
Ergasiphobia	Octaphonic	Hydropathy
Discombobulate	Pellucid	Petrology
Alopecia	Febrifacient	Patrology
Balderdash	Ultramontane	Odynophobia
Abstemious	Verrucose	Entomostracan
Confabulate	Szxicolous	Melanesia
Consanguineous	Hahoo	Onychophorous
Decalogue	Hebitate	Onychophaist
Diurnal	Lucifagus	Somnolent
Dactylogram	Pandiculation	Sinecure
Erdapfel	Sermoination	Nidificate
Kopophobia	Stentarophonic	Piscivorous
Acerebral	Tatterdemalion	Obsequious
Jobation	Thermanasthesia	Sobriquet
Lethonomia	Vellicate	

❖

Greek and Latin for Ten-Year-Olds

During the last two months of the school year, twice a week for about a half-hour each day, I introduced the children to the Greek and Latin origins of many of our English words. Below is a sampling of the Greek and Latin vocabulary the children learned. The format below is the exact same format used in the classroom. I would introduce the words using my laptop and LCD projector. Students had special etymology notebooks for taking notes and recording our discussions.

Amnesia

   a — without

   mne — remember

   sia — state of

Analysis

   ana — up, again

   ly — release

   sis — action of, or the act

Anatomy

   ana — again

   tom — cut

   y — state or quality

Arctic

    arc — bear

    tic — pertaining to

Asterisk

    aster — star

    isk — little

Atom

    a — not

    tom — cut

Chlorine

    chlor — yellow-green

    ine — chemical ending

Diameter

    dia — through

    met — measure

    e — English ending

Eccentric

    ec — out

    cen — common

t — agent

ic — pertaining to

Embryo

em — in

bry — grow

o — ending

Energy

en — in

erg — work

y — state

Geography

ge — earth

o — connector

graphy — to write

ic — pertaining to

Microscope

micro — small

o — connector

scop — to look or see

e — ending

Parallel

par — beside

allel — each other

Pediatrics

ped — child

iatr — doctor

ics — study of

Periscope

peri — around

scop — look at

e — ending

Psychology

psych — mind or soul

log — thought

y — state or quality

o — connector

Psychroaesthesia (unusual word that children love to lean)

psychr — cold

aesthe — feeling

sia — state or quality

(a state or condition of feeling cold when you are not)

Pyromania

pyr — fire

man — to be crazy

ia — suffix, state, or disease

o — connector

Rhinoceros

rhin — nose

o — connector

cer — horn, wax, or carotene

os — Latin ending

Telepathy

tele — far off

path — feel or feeling

y — state or quality

Telephone

tele — far off

phon — to speak or voice

e — ending

Telescope

tele — far off

scop — look at

e — ending

❖

Fiddling-Around Stories

Christmas Mouse

It was the night before Christmas, when all through the house,

One creature was stirring. It was a little black mouse.

It scampered through the cupboards looking for food, when it suddenly heard,

"Wake up, dude!

The presents are here, the presents are here, from Santa, his elf, and all the reindeer."

One by one the people raced downstairs, opening their presents and their stockings with absolutely no care.

Everything was strewn about the house with abandon, while the little black mouse looked with surprise upstairs.

And so it grew dark and quiet, and then the day turned into night, and the little black mouse had the whole house to himself.

—Cameron Croft

My Cat Boo

Boo the cat is really fun.

He likes to be outside in the sun.

He runs and jumps on moles in the ground

And makes a move at every sound.

—Melissa Morris

Joy

Joy is skipping along the beautiful meadow, delighted by the gorgeous violets gleaming in the sunlight. Joy loves to frolic in the tall grass. Joy is glad to be well and living. She is a tender, gracious girl full of enjoyment and glee. Joy is grateful for everything she has, because she is a very good-hearted girl. Joy is wearing a vivid pink dress, and a pretty blue bow in her brown, flowing hair. She slowly picks the violets one by one and puts them in her hair. As the sun goes to sleep in its orange and pink cloud bed, Joy must hurry home to look at the stars.

—Tori Webb

Flonkenberry

Flonkenberry is very scary, and you'd be scared if you saw him.

If you see him, you're toast, and if you live, don't boast, because he'll be back and you'll be his snack and won't stay alive like most.

—Isaac Kranz

Legal

I ate pie, got arrested.

Stopped moving, got a ticket.

Went outside, got imprisoned.

I stole a car, got one million dollars.

Ate the teacher's apple, got extra recess.

Stayed out after dark,

Got to play in the park.

—Jordan Meyer

Hair

Red and curly,

Brown or straight,

Hair is excellent.

Hair is great.

But when your hair is tangled

Or is in your face,

Your hair can

Be a

Disgrace.

—Rylee Wrenner

Ryan

My brother Ryan can drive you up the wall with his craziness. Ryan is a three-year-old who has the ocean's blueness in his eyes and the sun's brightness in his golden hair. Ryan loves to play with trucks. When you try to read or do your homework, all you hear are the sounds of trucks running all through the house. Ryan is also a loud person and loves to yell and scream with all his might. He has a lot of energy and gets it all out by dancing and yelling. Ryan is an adorable child when you give him bubblegum or a treat. Even though Ryan is a really annoying little brother, overall, Ryan can be a lovable and kind boy.

—Amber Giroux

APPENDIX L

❖

The Life-World

Each teacher has his or her own distinct life-world, which is the source of the teacher's interpretation of classroom reality. This world can be defined as the primary root of our thinking. To understand the life-world of the two elementary school teachers I studied and interviewed for my Doctoral Dissertation, I had to assume a natural attitude—becoming interested in the qualities and properties as experienced by these teachers. I'm trying to uncover the hidden acts of consciousness that are at the root of their behavior. My basic assumption is that these teachers' behavior cannot be separated from their own consciousness. What they are trying to do is based on an assumption that some type of reaction will take place. Below is Professor Frank Stone's conceptualization of Edmund Husserl's life-world.

Stratum One—This is the teacher's world of private experience, which is the deepest of the life-world strata. This can only be understood by exploring the teacher's deepest attitudes.

Stratum Two—This is a teacher's taken-for-granted world, which includes the ideas, premises, knowledge, and techniques the teacher assumes to be true or factual.

Stratum Three—This is the teacher's world of intersubjectivity. Here lie the values, intentions, and motives of the teacher's behavior. What I focused on were the rules, beliefs, and traditions these teachers conformed to.

Stratum Four—This is the teacher's world of interpersonal experiences. Included are the many teacher-student and teacher-teacher interactions.

Stratum Five—This is the teacher's world of reflections about his or her thoughts about and actions regarding teaching.

APPENDIX M

❖

Silly Putty and Other Polymers

Instant Glop

Materials

1 ultra-absorbent diaper
1 Ziploc plastic bag
About 50 ml water
1 5-oz. paper cup
Salt

Steps to Follow

1. Obtain an ultra-absorbent diaper.
2. Cut the diaper into one—or two-inch strips.
3. Place the strips in the Ziploc bag, seal, and shake well.
4. Open the Ziploc bag and remove the diaper and any loose cotton; save the powder.
5. Transfer the powder to the 5-oz. paper cup.
6. Add about 50 ml water. Observe.
7. Touch the solution in the paper cup. Describe what you see and feel.
8. Now place some of the Instant Glop in a paper cup. Add a small amount of salt. What happens?
   —Adapted from David Katz, *Investigations in Chemistry*

Monster Flesh

You can make a disgusting, gross monster and then sizzle the flesh off its bones.

Materials

1 c. flour
½ c. salt
1 tsp. alum
2 Tbsp. vegetable oil
½ c. water
Food coloring
Large bowl
1 plastic Ziploc bag
Lemon juice
Baking soda
Small toy figure skeleton

Steps to Follow

1. Mix the flour, salt, and alum together in the mixing bowl.
2. Add vegetable oil and mix well.
3. Add 8-10 drops of food coloring, and stir.
4. Add water a little bit at a time, mixing well.
5. Continue to add water until the material feels like dough.
6. Store the monster flesh in the plastic Ziploc bag.
7. Take some of your monster flesh and mix it with some baking soda.
8. Knead it well and add water if it gets too dry.
9. Take your small figure toy skeleton and apply the monster flesh to the entire surface.
10. If you want to dissolve the flesh off the monster, measure 1 tsp. lemon juice and add it to about 8 oz. water. Stir well.
11. Pour the liquid over your monster, and watch it sizzle.
    —Adapted from David Katz, *Investigations in Chemistry*

Rubber

You will need to order liquid latex from a science catalog.

Materials

About 20 ml liquid latex
Graduated cylinder
20 ml vinegar
2 paper cups
Spoon or stirring rod
Source of water
Small bucket to hold water

Steps to Follow

1. Measure about 20 ml of latex into a paper cup.
2. Pour a few drops into the palm of your hand and spread it out using your fingers. Describe its properties.
3. Pour about 20 ml vinegar into another paper cup.
4. Dip your spoon or stirring rod into the vinegar, and then into the latex, and then into the vinegar again. Remove the solidified latex and stretch it. Describe this polymer.
5. Add about 20 ml water to the latex, and stir the mixture. What happens?
6. Pour about 20 ml vinegar into the cup of latex and stir the mixture. Describe what happens.
7. Remove the mass from the cup and stirring rod with your fingers. Carefully squeeze the mass while washing it under water, preferably into a small bucket. Form the mass into a ball. Dry it with a paper towel. Drop the mass on the floor and describe what happens.
    —Adapted from David Katz, *Investigations in Chemistry*

Slime

The original Slime is a product of the Mattel Toy Corporation. You will be making slime using polyvinyl alcohol, borax, and food coloring.

Materials

About 20 ml polyvinyl alcohol
Popsicle sticks
Food coloring
Balance
Water
5 ml 4-5% borax solution. Make this solution a day ahead of time. To make this solution, weigh out 5 g borax and 95 g water. Mix together.

Steps to Follow

1. Pour about 20 ml polyvinyl solution into a paper cup. Examine the solution with a Popsicle stick. Is it sticky?
2. Add one or two drops of food coloring. Stir.
3. Measure about 5 ml borax solution, pour it into the polyvinyl alcohol, and stir. What happens?
4. Remove the new material from the cup and knead it in your hand. The material will become firm and lose some of its stickiness.
5. Stretch the slime polymer. Roll the slime into a ball and drop it. What happens?
6. Place a small piece of slime on a tabletop. Hit it with your hand. What happens?
   —Adapted from David Katz, *Investigations in Chemistry*

Silly Putty

Silly Putty is a silicone polymer made in 1941 and marketed as a toy by Crayola. You are going to make your own silly putty.

Materials

25 ml Elmer's white glue
Paper cup
About 20 ml water
Food coloring
Graduated cylinder
Borax solution
Ziploc bag

Steps to Follow

1. Measure 25 ml Elmer's white glue into a paper cup.
2. Add 20 ml water and stir well.
3. Add about 5 drops of food coloring.
4. Add about 3 ml borax solution and stir well.
5. Pour off any extra liquid and remove your silly putty. It will be sticky for a few minutes.
6. Test your silly putty. Does it stretch? What happens when it is pulled hard? Does it bounce?
7. Store your silly putty in a Ziploc bag.
   —Adapted from David Katz, *Investigations in Chemistry*

The Ooze Ball

The ooze ball is an elastic non-Newtonian fluid that can be purchased in special stores. You will be making one.

Materials

Paper cup
1 tsp. talcum powder
Oil-free moisturizing lotion
Elmer's glue
Water
Food coloring
Borax solution

Steps to Follow

1. Measure 1 tsp. talcum power and place it in the paper cup.
2. Add 2 tsp. oil-free moisturizing lotion, 2 tsp. Elmer's glue, and 2 tsp. water, and stir well.
3. Add 3-5 drops food coloring.
4. Add 1 tsp. borax solution and stir well.
5. Remove your ooze ball from the cup. It will be sticky, but handle it and it should become less sticky. Store the ooze ball in a plastic bag.
6. If your ooze ball dries, add small amounts of the oil-free moisturize or wet it with water. If your ooze ball sticks to a rug, use soap and water to clean the rug.
   —Adapted from David Katz, *Investigations in Chemistry*

Monster Foam

To make monster foam, you will need to order containers of Craft Cast A and Craft Cast B from a science catalog.

Materials

Craft Cast A and B
Large paper cup
Popsicle stick or straw
Protective gloves
Safety goggles
Food coloring

Steps to Follow

1. While wearing safety goggles and plastic or rubber gloves, pour about 3 oz. Craft Cast A into the large paper cup. Into another cup, pour 3 oz. Craft Cast B.
2. Add food coloring to the Craft Cast A.
3. Now add Craft Cast B to Craft Cast A. Do *not* breathe in any of the vapor. And don't handle the chemicals.
4. Foam will start to form. Place a straw or Popsicle stick into the foam and observe.

APPENDIX N

❖

Founders Woods

A maple/beech forest is part of the Founders School's grounds. When I began working in Essex in 1985, I explored the woods and created a nature trail. Each year, all of my students explored the woods, drew scale maps including symbols for plants of the woods, collected and pressed plants, and learned the common and scientific names of twenty-seven plants. Below is a list of all the plants the students learned of.

1. American Beech — *Fagus grandifolia*
2. Beaked Hazel — *Corylus rostrata*
3. Black Birch — *Betula lenta*
4. Black Cherry — *Prunus serotina*
5. Blackberry — *Rubus allegheninsis*
6. Blueberry — *Vaccinium angustifolium*
7. Bracken Fern — *Pteridium aquilinum*
8. Clubmoss — *Lycopodium obscurum*
9. Eastern Hemlock — *Tsuga canadensis*
10. Eastern White Pine — *Pinus strobus*
11. Goldenrod — *Solidago*
12. Gray Birch — *Betula populifolia*
13. Hay-scented Fern — *Dennstaedtia punctilobula*
14. Japanese Honeysuckle — *Lonicera japonica*
15. Paper Birch — *Betula papyrifera*
16. Partridge Berry — *Mitchella repens*
17. Pipsissewa — *Chimaphila umbellata*
18. Raspberry — *Rubus strigosus*
19. Red Maple — *Acer rubrum*
20. Red Oak — *Quercus rubra*
21. Sarsaparilla — *Aralia nudicaulis*
22. Scots Pine — *Pinus sylvestris*
23. Sweet Fern — *Myrica asplenifolia*

Horace Puglisi

24. Trembling Aspen   *Populus tremuloides*
25. White Oak   *Quercus alba*
26. Wintergreen   *Gaultheria procumbens*
27. Witch Hazel   *Hamamelis virgiana*

APPENDIX O

❖

Books That Have Impacted My Teaching

Professional and Inspirational Books

Blindsided, Richard M. Cohen
Climate Process and Change, Edward Bryant
A Good Scent from a Strange Mountain, Robert Olen Butler
How the Brain Works, Leslie Hart
Jacob A. Riis: Photographer & Citizen, Alexander Alland Sr.
The Last Lecture, Randy Pausch
Mountains Beyond Mountains, Tracy Kidder
Plants, People, and Culture: The Science of Ethnobotany, Michael J. Balick and Paul Alan Cox
The Psychology of the Child, Jean Piaget
Schools without Failure, William Glaser
Tuesdays with Morrie, Mitch Albom
Unbroken, Laura Hillenbrand
A Whole New Mind, Daniel Pink

Selected Books Related to Teaching

1001 Questions Answered About: Hurricanes, Tornadoes and Other Natural Disasters, Barbara Tufty
Conceptual Physics, Paul G. Hewitt
Dictionary of Geological Terms, Robert L. Bates and Julia A. Jackson
Dictionary of Scientific Literacy, Richard P. Brennan
Ellis Island: Gateway to the American Dream, Pamela A. Reeves
Entertaining Mathematical Puzzles, Martin Gardner
The Environmental Sciences, Peter J. Bowler

Exploring Chemical Elements and Their Compounds, David L. Heiserman

Extraordinary Women Scientists, Darlene R. Stille

Galileo, James Reston Jr.

Glaciers, Michael Hambrey and Jürg Alean

Great Scientific Experiments, Rom Harré

Handbook of Nature Study, Anna Botsford Comstock

Hands on Meteorology, Zbigniew Sorbjan

Handy Space Answer Book, Phillis Engelbert and Diane L. Dupuis

The Historical Background of Chemistry, Henry M. Leicester

Historical Connections in Mathematics, volumes I, II, and III, Wilbert and Luetta Reimer

Human Anatomy and Physiology, David Le Vay

Ice Blink: The Tragic Fate of Sir John Franklin's Lost Polar Expedition, Scott Cookman

The Illustrated Dinosaur Dictionary, Helen Roney Sattler

Invitations to Science Inquiry, Tik L. Liem

The Joy of Mathematics, Theoni Pappas

Larousse Dictionary of Scientists, Hazel Muir

Lessons of the Rainforest, Suzanne Head and Robert Heinzman

Lewis & Clark: Voyage of Discovery, Sam Abell and Stephen E. Ambrose

Louis Pasteur: Free Lance of Science, René J. Dubos

Medicine Quest, Mark J. Plotkin, PhD

A Neotropical Companion, John C. Kricher

Our Changing Planet, Fred T. and Judith A. Mackenzie

Over the Edge of the World, Laurence Bergreen

Periodic Kingdom, P.W. Atkin

The Scientific Companion, Cesare Emiliani

The Shrub Identification Book, George W.D. Symonds

South, Sir Ernest Shackleton

The Sun's Heartbeat, Bob Berman

The Superior Person's Book of Words, Peter Bowler

Stone Walls and Sugar Maples, John Burk and Marjorie Holland

Tales of a Shaman's Apprentice, Mark J. Plotkin, PhD

The Tree Identification Book, George W.D. Symonds

The Triumph of Discovery: Women Scientists Who Won the Nobel Prize, Joan Dash

Understanding by Design: The Six Facets of Understanding, Grant Wiggins and Jay McTighe

Usborne Illustrated Dictionary of Chemistry, Jane Wertheim, Chris Oxlade, and Dr. John Waterhouse

Weather, B.W. Atkinson and Alan Gadd

The Weather Book, Ralph Hardy, Peter Wright, John Kingston, and John Gibbin

Wetland, Woodland, Wildland, Elizabeth H. Thompson and Eric R. Sorenson

Where Puddles Go: Investigating Science with Kids, Michael Strauss

Words You Should Know, David Olsen

Written in Stone, Chet and Maureen E. Raymo